THE PREPARATION OF CONTRACTS AND CONVEYANCES

THE MACMILLAN COMPANY
NEW YORK · BOSTON · CHICAGO · DALLAS
ATLANTA · SAN FRANCISCO

MACMILLAN & CO., LIMITED
LONDON · BOMBAY · CALCUTTA
MELBOURNE

THE MACMILLAN COMPANY
OF CANADA, LIMITED
TORONTO

The Preparation of
Contracts and Conveyances

With
Forms and Problems

BY
HENRY WINTHROP BALLANTINE

PROFESSOR OF LAW IN THE UNIVERSITY
OF MINNESOTA

New York
THE MACMILLAN COMPANY
1929

Printed in the United States of America by
THE FERRIS PRINTING COMPANY, NEW YORK

PREFACE

The practical suggestions and forms here given for the preparation of legal documents are not intended to enable the business man, the banker or the notary to draw documents or to dispense with competent legal advice. They are intended primarily for the law student for study and the lawyer for ready reference, but they should also be useful to the student of business law and the business man as a warning of the pitfalls which beset him in business transactions and the precautions that should be taken. No book has heretofore been prepared as a basis for a course in the drafting and criticism of actual business forms. Simple forms, problems and exercises are given as materials for practice.

The only effective way to learn the art of drafting is by practical exercises which require the actual preparation of the various sorts of contracts, notes, deeds, wills, mortgages, leases and other documents in everyday use. Exercises in the organization of corporations, partnerships and business trusts and in the examination of abstracts of title are also given.

The idea is to give a series of concise, practical suggestions and directions as to what to do and what to avoid, rather than to discuss the law of the subject. A glance at the book will serve as a reminder of important points to be covered at the critical moment when an instrument is being drawn up or a printed form considered.

The book may be used as an adjunct to courses in business law, as well as a basis for courses in drafting documents in law schools. It aims to give that aspect of business law that the business man most needs to study—the practical application of the lessons of legal experience and foresight to the transaction of business.

Many law graduates, upon entering practice, find great difficulty in applying their knowledge to the skillful drafting of important papers, and are in danger of making serious mistakes and of inflicting great loss upon their clients.

The younger members of the bar who have not yet acquired facility in drafting documents as a result of experience in practice, and who have not had a course in this work, may thus find the book useful for study and reference.

H. W. BALLANTINE.

University of Minnesota,
February, 1921.

TABLE OF CONTENTS

THE PREPARATION OF CONTRACTS
AND CONVEYANCES

THE PREPARATION OF CONTRACTS AND CONVEYANCES

CHAPTER I

GENERAL DIRECTIONS FOR DRAFTING CONTRACTS AND CONVEYANCES

The Skill Required.—Some business transactions are fairly simple and follow customary forms which the parties themselves may be competent to prepare; but in all important matters it is indeed hazardous to draft or execute contracts or conveyances without skilled legal assistance. The attorney's fee is a small price to pay for insurance against subsequent trouble and litigation. Advise with the lawyer *before* signing the contract rather than afterward.

One cannot rely upon the adverse party not to take unfair advantage in drawing a contract. Printed forms of contracts are generally so drawn as to give undue protection to those who have them printed; thus land contracts and leases are usually drawn with stringent provisions in favor of the sellers or landlords who have most to do with the business, and who aim to keep the upper hand.

In drafting legal documents one must have sufficient knowledge of the law relating to the subject to know what are the requisites and formalities prescribed by law, and what are the dangers and pitfalls to be provided against. Before undertaking to prepare an instrument, the draftsman should inform himself on the

1

statutes and decisions of the particular state as to the formalities and other points of law governing the transaction. He must know the effect of technical legal terms. He must be skillful in expressing himself clearly and concisely. He must have sufficient experience and familiarity with the subject matter of the business in hand to be able to foresee how the transaction will work out, step by step, in a practical way.

If all contracts were drawn by highly skilled lawyers or perhaps even by experienced business men, not nearly so much litigation would result. The skilled draftsman would think the transaction out so carefully, and would so fully and clearly prescribe what was to be done that all contingencies would be provided for. The average person, in the usual informal contract, expresses the agreement in a careless, general way, assuming that the other party will do the right thing, and does not bother to take care of difficulties that may arise.

The Plan of the Transaction.—The first step toward the preparation of a legal document is to obtain full information as to the facts upon which the draftsman is to work. It is often difficult to ascertain just what the parties want, as they may not be fully agreed, or know only in a general way what it is they wish to accomplish. The draftsman must not only ascertain the general scheme and purpose of the transaction, but he must be able to devise the form and methods by which it may best be carried out. Having got all the information before him in the shape of memoranda instructions and documents, he should ponder how the result which his client desires may be accomplished most safely and directly. The object and design of the transaction must be clearly conceived first of all. The draftsman is a legal architect and should form an outline of the framework of the instrument. It is usually advisable to sketch out a plan on paper, tabulating the principal points in one, two, three order. He should go over the different steps that each party is to take one by one, and consider as to each what might interfere with it and how to guard against mishaps or complications. Books of forms and precedents should be perused in search of provisions and clauses that may be adapted to the purpose. He must seek reasonable protection, but should not frighten away the other party by needlessly severe restrictions and conditions.

The one who drafts a contract for the other party to sign has an important strategical advantage, but the draft is apt to be rejected, unless it expresses his intentions and expectations fairly. Inexperienced and careless draftsmen will often fail to include in a document important provisions and safeguards, or leave vital points uncertain and vague, which may result in loss and years of expensive litigation.

Often-times contracts must be prepared with reference to the willingness of those who are to sign them to agree to their terms, and sometimes it will be difficult to get a party to sign a contract with long and somewhat involved provisions, however just and plain they may be, as he will feel that he does not understand them, and will suspect that some undue advantage is being taken of him.

Working Out Details.—In important matters each side should be represented by its own attorney, but often-times one lawyer serves for all, and it will be his duty to see that neither party takes any advantage of the other. Let us suppose that two men, a vendor and a purchaser of land, come to the same lawyer to have a contract of sale drawn up to protect them both. The matter of price is the principal item in their minds. They will probably be vague on the details of how the business will be carried through and will expect the lawyer to suggest the various matters to be provided for. He should visualize in his imagination the practical working out of the transaction, step by step. Some of the questions which the draftsman will ask of the parties, in order to bring them into agreement on all matters, are as follows:

Land Contract.—What is the exact description of the property? Who is to furnish an abstract of title? What time is to be allowed for examination of the record title, for making objections thereto and for curing possible defects? Who is to have possession of the property until the day fixed for completion? If the purchaser fails to pay the price promptly, is he to forfeit all rights under the contract? How shall the purchaser be protected against loss by fire pending the completion of the contract? Is the title to be taken subject to building restrictions and easements contained in prior deeds, if any such exist? When and where shall the deed be delivered and the price be paid? May it be paid by check? Is the purchaser to assume a mortgage or other lien on the property? These matters will be found dealt with in the chapter on Land Contracts.

Logging Contract.—Suppose it is a logging contract which the parties desire to make in which the logger is to cut and purchase the timber on the owner's land. What is to be cut? Is the logger to enter and cut into sawlogs only "merchantable" pine and hardwood timber growing on the land during a certain logging season? What trees and what sizes of trees are to be cut? What about rights of way to and from the land? Where are the logs to be delivered? Is the buyer to have the right to change the place of delivery? How are they to be marked and scaled? What is to be done with the branches and tops? When and where is the price to be paid? Is the title to remain in the seller until the logs are paid for? What is to happen in case of such an accident as a forest fire? Are the huts of lumbermen to be built of logs or out of boards and tar paper? Is necessary firewood to be paid for? What is to happen in case of breach of contract by either party?

Form Books.—When all these terms and details are settled, they should be arranged in logical order and expressed in a clear-cut and lawyer-like manner. The various standard collections of business forms and precedents, some of which are general and some adapted to particular states, are often very helpful in suggesting the customary clauses and provisions to be employed. (See Jones, Legal Forms; Tiffany's Legal and Business Forms.) Without the use of form books and precedents it is almost impossible to avoid overlooking some points of a contract or conveyance which ought to be covered. These ready-made forms are however always more or less ill-adapted and unreliable and must be used with great care and circumspection.

Care and Foresight.—The object of a legal instrument such as a contract is to map out a more or less complex business transaction which may affect the welfare and legal relations of the parties for years to come, and which is subject to all the risks of human misfortune and perversity. The general object of the transaction the draftsman may obtain from the parties; the details of the plan he will have to study out for himself with a view to accomplishing the object in the best way. The greatest care must be taken to force a complete agreement, to provide for untoward contingencies, and to leave no occasion for future dispute. After the contract is drafted, it must be revised, criticized and tested in all its parts, so that there will be no occasion for a subsequent lawsuit.

Safeguards and Qualifications.—One entering into a contract should carefully weigh and consider what he is willing to bind himself to do and limit the scope of his promises accordingly. A person who draws a contract cleverly will put in strict conditions qualifying his own liability, but will try to make the promise on the other side, as unconditional as possible. Take an insurance policy, for instance. There is a promise to pay insurance money in large print on the first page, but there are a great many stringent conditions and qualifications in smaller print on the following pages which limit the promise to pay, and which the insured has to accept, whether he likes them or not. These qualifications are worth a great deal to the insurance company.

Keeping Control.—Contracts are continually made in which one or both parties rely as to details on the honesty and good nature of the other party and his willingness to perform his contract and do the right thing, but it is well to remember that his sense of business integrity and fair dealing may become warped by temper, business difficulties or the disadvantageous working of the transaction.

The draftsman should consider carefully what is to happen if either party defaults or dies or becomes unable to perform; or if the property involved should perish or be accidentally damaged or destroyed. He should leave as little as possible to the good faith or good nature of the other party. He should extend no more credit than is necessary, and so far as negotiations permit, part with no money or title to property except upon the condition of receiving at the same time, or before, its equivalent. He will hedge about his promises with exceptions and conditions. He will thus keep control of the transaction, and by an ounce of precaution and foresight may prevent serious losses and legal complications.

Covering Contingencies.—Laymen are apt to be exceedingly hasty, rash, and uncritical in the preparation of serious legal documents which embody transactions involving the gravest risks of future complications. They do not realize that impossibility of performance of a contract is often no excuse, and that untoward contingencies should be provided for and in such terms as to furnish proper safeguards against possible future difficulties. The best place to prevent litigation is at the source. It is better to make a long clear contract which covers with considerable particularity every step in the transaction than a short "simple" one that leaves the parties unprepared for trouble.

Skeleton Outline of a Contract.—It may be of service to give a skeleton outline indicating in a general way matters which should be considered in drawing every contract.

1. Caption, with place, date and names of parties. (A. B. and C. D. do hereby agree as follows):
2. Explanatory recitals as to object of transaction.
3. Formal recital of consideration.
4. State what A. B. promises to do.
5. State what C. D. promises to do; in each case with all details of time, place, and manner of performance.
6. Indicate in connection with the promises or separately the various conditions to or the excuses from performance, such as impossibility, breach by the other party, and so forth.
7. Provide, if possible, remedies in case of breach, such as liquidated damages and attorneys' fees.

8. Signatures of the parties, and sometimes their seals.

9. In some cases, certificate of acknowledgment.

It is well to devote a separate paragraph to each item of the contract, in order to deal with it fully and completely, and in order that it may be less easily overlooked when it comes to performance. The contract should either include the whole agreement, or else recite that the writing is not complete. By the so-called "parol evidence rule," a written contract will be presumed to contain the entire agreement of the parties and to merge all prior negotiations. A recital of receipt of consideration should invariably be inserted. The different parts of a contract will now be discussed more specifically.

Commencement.—The formal commencement of a contract reads: "This Agreement made this ...... day of................, 1920, between Adam Bede, party of the first part, and Noah Williams, party of the second part, Witnesseth as follows." Instead of using the general term "Agreement" or "Indenture," the particular kind of instrument, lease, mortgage, contract of sale, etc., may be designated. The contract may simply commence: "It is hereby agreed between "A. B. and C. D. as follows."

The parties should be accurately described by their full names, not by their initials merely. Their residences and occupations may well be added for purposes of identification in conveyances which will have to be referred to in tracing title many years later. Instead of designating the parties as parties of the first, second or third part, they may be more conveniently named as "Owner," "Vendor," "Purchaser," "Lender," "Borrower," such descriptive titles being given them in the caption. In case a partnership is a party, the names of the individual partners should always be given, as well as the firm name under which they transact business. In case a corporation is a party, it is well that the state of its incorporation and principal place of business should be given. Agents should make contracts in the name of the principal, not in their own names. A married woman should use her own Christian name, stating that she is the wife of so and so.

It is customary in documents relating to the conveyance of property, such as deeds, contracts of sale, mortgages, and leases, that the name of the conveying parties be placed first. In building, construction, and employment contracts, the name of the owner or employer usually is placed first. It is not necessary to repeat in each paragraph "It is hereby further expressly agreed by the parties hereto, for themselves, their executors, administrators, heirs, and assigns, etc." A clause may be inserted at the beginning or end, once for all, to the effect that "This contract shall extend to and be binding upon the parties, their personal representatives, successors, and assigns,"—thus saving wearisome repetition. So also, words of promise and mutual agreement need not be again and again repeated.

Arrangement.—The contract should be arranged, as far as possible, in some systematic and logical order. The document may well be cast into separate numbered paragraphs for convenience of reference, each paragraph dealing with some one aspect or phase of the transaction. The document may commence with recitals briefly setting forth the facts as to situation of the parties and the purpose to be accomplished by the transaction, as an aid to construing the contract, and with a recital of the receipt of consideration. General provisions for arbitration, liquidated damages, and attorneys' fees will naturally be reserved until the end.

Definiteness.—The acts which each party is required to perform should be stated as clearly and definitely as possible, with the time, place, manner, and order of performance. Vague terms, such as *"fair," "proper,"* and *"reasonable,"* should be avoided and definite standards of excellence, fairness, and reasonableness should be provided in advance. Sometimes these are left to the certificate of an architect or engineer. The precise acts or things which are expected should be defined, leaving nothing open to doubt or subsequent agreement. For the sake of clearness and simplicity use terse, short, blunt sentences and break up long sentences and paragraphs into short ones. Different terms should not be used to refer to the same thing in different parts of the instrument; nor should the same words or phrases be employed with different meanings. When a person or thing has once been mentioned, reference may thereafter be made to the "said" or "aforesaid" person or thing as an aid to brevity and certainty.

Execution.—Agreements should be signed, when practicable, by all the parties to them, or by their authorized agents. A document which concludes with such words as "Witness our hands" would be *prima facie* incomplete if unsigned by any of the parties mentioned in the body of the contract. The so-called testimonium clause at the end of the contract usually reads, "In Witness Whereof, the parties hereto have hereunto set their hands the day and year first above written," or "Witness our hands and seals this .... day of August, 1916.

"John Doe   (Seal)

"Richard Roe,   (Seal)

"By John Smith, Agent.

"Signed in the presence of:

....

....

       "Witness."

If the signatures are to be witnessed, the witnesses sign in the above blanks. If there is to be a guarantor, this form may be added:

GUARANTY

In consideration of one dollar in hand paid, I do hereby guarantee to said John Doe that the said Richard Roe will faithfully perform the above contract.

Or,

For value received, the undersigned hereby guarantees the payment or performance of the within contract, and agrees to pay all costs, expenses and attorneys' fees incurred in enforcing the same.

An agreement made by an agent should be expressed throughout to be made in the name of the principal and agent should sign the principal's name *by* himself as agent—e. g., "A. B. by C. D., Agent." If he executes in his own name, he may incur personal liability on the contract.

Acknowledgment of Execution and Attestation.— Acknowledgment of the signature before a notary public is unnecessary, except for the purpose of recording of deeds, mortgages and contracts affecting the title to land. The certificate of acknowledgment is often made by statute *prima facie* evidence of the execution of the instrument, and will permit it to be offered in evidence without further proof of the signature of the party.

It is well that the delivery of a deed, especially deeds of gift, to take full effect at the death of the grantor, should be made by the grantor in the presence of two or more witnesses, and that a memorandum of the delivery should be made and attested upon the deed. Whether or not a deed or sealed instrument was ever put into effect will often depend upon the testimony of witnesses and presumptions, which result in uncertainty and litigation.

It is not essential that the signature of the parties should be attested by a witness, except in wills, and in some States in the case of deeds, leases and contracts which are to be recorded. If an attested signature is to be proved in court, the law requires the attesting witness to be produced or his absence to be accounted for. It is thus sometimes more difficult to prove a signature which is witnessed than one which is not. The latter may be proved by anybody who saw the signature affixed or who is familiar with the handwriting of the party and his signature generally, so that he can identify the signature in question as genuine. If you have your attesting witness within reach and he is reliable and well-known, his testimony would be more convincing in a case of dispute than that of one who merely recognizes the signer's handwriting. It might cause inconvenience, however, to have an attesting witness if he could not be found and produced when needed. Where an illiterate person signs by mark, a witness should attest the agreement as having been read over to him, and certify that he made his mark in the presence of the witness.

The Advisability of Having a Seal.—If there is consideration for the respective promises, a seal is not necessary to a contract; but a seal, even if it is no more than a scroll of the pen, has the beneficial effect under many statutes of extending the period of the limitation of actions. If a corporation is a party, it is well to have the corporate seal, as this is prima facie evidence of the authority of the officers to execute the contract on behalf of the corporation. One should remember that in case of suit on a contract executed by an agent, his authority as agent will have to be proved in some other way than by his own declarations. All conveyances ordinarily require a seal.

PRACTICAL SUGGESTIONS ON THE MAKING OF CONTRACTS

1. Put all contracts in writing as far as possible. Consult an attorney in any important transaction. Don't leave business matters to oral understandings, loosely written letters or rough and general estimates.

2. Don't rely on oral representations of salesmen, agents, and brokers. Insert all the representations, conditions, and understandings in the contract itself. Remember the parol evidence rule.

3. To convert an offer into a valid contract it is essential that the acceptance be absolute and unconditional. A counter-proposition which varies from the offer is a rejection.

4. Avoid haste. Take time and thought for the preparation of contracts. Plan out clearly what you want in advance and how it will work out step by step, and insert your expectations definitely and fully. Make an outline sketch before attempting to draft the instrument.

5. Printed provisions on letter-heads may or may not be regarded as part of the contract. This depends on whether they are referred to and incorporated in the body of the letter.

6. Modifications of contracts and extensions of time should be reduced to writing, recite a consideration, and be signed by both parties, preferably under seal.

7. Provide in the agreement for suspension or excuse of performance in case of interruptions caused by war, strikes, labor troubles, floods, fire, stoppage of water supply, acts of God, or any cause beyond the control of the parties preventing or delaying or hindering the carrying out of the contract. Unforeseen difficulties or even impossibility of performance are often no excuse unless it is so provided in the contract.

8. Make prompt payment or punctual delivery of

installments a condition precedent to the right of the other party to require further performance on your part.

9. Don't leave the evidence of the contract entirely in the hands of the other party. Keep a copy or duplicate of all contracts.

10. In the case of contracts to be performed partly in two or more States, indicate the State whose laws shall control the interpretation, performance, and obligation of the contract.

11. Provide for protection in case of suit over use of patented articles and devices.

12. If a contract made by an agent is subject to approval of the principal, it does not become binding on either party until approved by the principal.

13. Make inquiry in regard to persons with whom you intend to contract from banks and credit agencies before having dealings with them involving any credit or reliance upon their representations. Don't send money to persons you don't know about, trusting to them to send you securities or goods in return. If you must deal with persons of unknown or doubtful character or responsibility, take unusual care to keep matters in your own hands and control.

14. Don't make contracts where the other party, owing to inexperience or incompetence, will find the business unprofitable or will probably fail to do his part.

Perform promptly on your own side and prepare to perform in ample season.

15. Don't sign any contract without reading and understanding its terms. You are bound by the fine-print provisions in documents which you accept whether you read them or not.

16. Consider all contingencies that may arise, and provide carefully for them in advance.

Employment Contracts.—Employment contracts are of various sorts and degrees of importance, but there are certain matters which it is desirable to provide for in drafting important ones.

1. In the first place the duties to be performed by the employee should be duly specified. Reasonable elasticity should be allowed so that the employee shall be bound to perform such duties in the general line of employment as the employer may direct.

2. The employee should agree to devote his entire time, skill and attention to the said employment, and to render diligent and skillful service. The standard of skill and excellence is difficult to define, but he may be required to perform the duties or services to the entire satisfaction and approval of the employer. It is common to provide that, if the employee fails to perform the services to the satisfaction of the employer, the latter shall have the option to terminate the contract upon certain notice.

3. The duration of the employment or period of service together with the date of beginning should be clearly specified.

4. Provision should be made allowing the employer to terminate the contract in case of the interruption of his business. It may be provided that the contract shall immediately cease upon the death or incapacity for business of either party, or upon the employer ceasing to carry on the said business or becoming bankrupt.

5. The compensation or salary will probably be made payable by the week, month, or year. Regular hours and overtime. Share in profits, if any.

6. The effect of absence, death or sickness of the employee should also be specified: (1) as to compensation; (2) as to continuance of employment.

7. The employer may expressly reserve the right of dismissal of the employee for unexcused absence, serious illness, inattention to business, incompetence, carelessness, intoxication, immoral or disrespectful conduct, or violation of rules and regulations. It may be expressly agreed that the employee shall observe and follow all reasonable directions and instructions of the employer. Frequently the employer reserves the right to terminate the employment arbitrarily upon two weeks' written notice.

8. It is often advisable to provide that the employee shall not enter into competition with the employer during or after the contract, and shall not use or disclose trade secrets or information concerning the business or affairs of the employer.

9. The employee may well procure a promise from the employer to furnish reasonable opportunity to work, especially where the amount of compensation depends on the amount of work performed.

Contracts of employment between managers and singers or actors are sometimes very elaborate and stringent. In the theatrical business many irresponsible people are engaged, and it is felt by managers that they must be held with a strong hand for the protection of the employer. A requisition for a contract between manager and actor will be given as an exercise in drafting. (For forms of such a contract, see Tiffany's Legal and Business Forms, chapter 35, p. 1223; 2 Ely, Property and Contract, pp. 737, 740.)

REQUISITION FOR CONTRACT OF EMPLOYMENT BETWEEN MANAGER AND ACTOR OR ACTRESS

Prepare a contract of employment between a theatrical manager and performer covering the following points:

1. Recital of intended production, to begin on or about a certain date.

2. Duties of the performer to sing or perform to the best of his ability, to attend rehearsals, to know his part or character.

3. Duration of employment and working hours.

4. Compensation; deductions which may be made.

5. Effect of calamity or cause rendering performances impossible, or abandonment of the production for any reason.

6. Effect of illness or absence of performer.

7. Restrictions on performance elsewhere without consent of manager.

8. Costumes, to be furnished by performer or manager.

9. Option to cancel on two weeks' notice by manager.

10. Execution by the parties.

Example for Study and Criticism.—The following form of employment contract of a designer of men's clothes by a clothing manufacturer as set forth in De Zeichner v. Lamm & Co. (187 Ill. App. 25) is submitted for study and criticism.[1]

Agreement made and entered into this first day of June, A. D., 1911, by and between Lamm & Company, an Illinois corporation doing business in the City of Chicago, party of the first part, and Mayer J. De Zeichner, now of the City of Chicago, party of the second part:

WHEREAS, the party of the first part is engaged in the business of manufacturing and dealing in men's clothing, and has a factory at the City of Chicago, and is desirous of employing the party of the second part as a designer and manufacturer, and

Whereas, the party of the second part is a designer and manufacturer of men's clothing and is desirous of entering the employ of the party of the first part,

NOW, THEREFORE, THIS AGREEMENT WIT-

NESSETH: That for and in consideration of the sum of One Dollar, lawful money of the United States, the receipt whereof is hereby acknowledged, and in further consideration of the mutual covenants and conditions hereinafter expressed, the parties to these presents agree:

FIRST: The party of the first part hereby engages the services of the party of the second part as a designer and manufacturer in the business conducted by it for a period of one year from the date of this agreement, that is to say up to May 31, 1912, and for such further time as is hereinafter provided for.

SECOND: The party of the second part hereby accepts such employment and agrees to devote his entire time, skill, energy and attention and the best of his ability as such designer and manufacturer in the business of the party of the first part.

THIRD: The party of the second part, during the time of his said employment, shall have full and exclusive charge of the mechanical branch of the business of the party of the first part; shall have full and exclusive charge of the designing and cutting and manufacturing of the men's clothing; shall originate the styles and designs, and in creating styles shall take into consideration the suggestions as to weave and style made by the party of the first part.

FOURTH: The party of the first part shall furnish to the party of the second part all facilities required by the party of the second part in the performance of his said duties, and the party of the second part shall have full and exclusive authority to engage or discharge such employees as may be necessary to be employed in the manufacturing department of the party of the second part, due regard always being had to the welfare and best interests of the party of the first part.

FIFTH: As and for compensation for the services so to b rendered by the party of the second part to the party of the first part, the party of the first part agrees to pay to the party of the second part the sum of Ten Thousand Dollars ($10,000.00) per annum, payable in equal monthly installments of Eight Hundred Thirty-three Dollars and Thirty-three Cents ($833.33) on the first day of each month, the first installment to be paid to the party of the second part the first day of July, 1911.

SIXTH: The party of the second part shall be allowed vacation for a period not exceeding two weeks in the aggregate, whenever the condition of the business of the party of the first part may warrant his so taking vacation. No deduction is to be made from the salary of the party of the second part on account of such vacation.

SEVENTH: At the expiration of the term of one year, the said employment shall not terminate, but this agreement shall continue in force and effect thereafter, subject, however, to the right of either party to terminate said employment by giving to the other party three months' previous notice in writing of its or his intention so to terminate the same, and said employment shall terminate at the end of three months from the time of giving notice.

IN WITNESS WHEREOF, the parties have set their hands and seals.

Lamm & Company (Seal)

Mayer J. De Zeichner (Seal)

---

[1]Note—It would be well to include in the contract a power in the employer to discharge the employee for incompetency in case his services were not satisfactory, and for release of the employer in case of destruction of the factory or other suspension of business. This contract does not adequately protect the employer.

CHAPTER II

PREPARATION OF NEGOTIABLE INSTRUMENTS

Notes, Drafts and Checks.—Negotiable instruments perform a very useful function in credit and business transactions. There is no other form of contract so well standardized or which expresses in so few words the rights and liabilities of the parties as negotiable paper. If the standard forms are departed from, very close questions as to the effect on the negotiability of the instrument may arise. While as between the immediate parties negotiability does not matter, this is a feature of great importance if the document is intended to circulate freely or to be discounted by a bank. A purchaser of negotiable paper without notice takes it free from all "equities" or personal defenses between the original parties, such as fraud, payments not indorsed on the note or lack or failure of consideration. Only those provisions of the law will be referred to here which affect the preparation of these contracts.

A negotiable promissory note in the ordinary form is as follows:

$1,000.00   Chicago, Ill.,
                                              Sept. 1, 1920.

On demand (or 60 days or 3 months after date) for value received I promise to pay Richard Roe, or order (or to the order of Richard Roe) at the First National Bank, the sum of one thousand dollars ($1,000) with interest at the rate of six per cent per annum, payable quarterly.

(Signed)   John Doe

By Mary Doe, Agent.

In this note Joe Doe is maker, Mary Doe is his agent, and Richard Roe is payee.

Negotiability.—Is it advisable to put notes and checks in negotiable form? If one is taking a note from the maker and is to hold it and collect it himself, the negotiable form is not important as the non-negotiable note is a perfectly valid and enforcible contract. But if one wishes to sell or discount the note, or if one is buying from some one who is not the maker and wishes to be sure that he can force the maker to pay it, the negotiable form is a matter of great importance.

A purchaser of a note or draft runs some risks in cashing, discounting or buying even negotiable instruments, but he does not run nearly so many risks as if the instrument is non-negotiable. On the other hand, the maker of such a negotiable instrument may be deprived of certain just defenses to payment as a consequence of putting such a document into circulation.

The debtor, the man who is drawing commercial paper, will of course best protect himself by putting it in non-negotiable form, thus preserving possible defenses as against future purchasers. Thus, if it is agreed that a certified check for one thousand dollars ($1,000) is to be deposited with a manufacturer to be held until one thousand dollars worth of goods is shipped, it would be advisable to let the check contain the agreement that it is not to be cashed until the goods are shipped according to the order. This will render it non-negotiable and protect the buyer. In general, the debtor should, if possible, make notes and drafts payable by him at a future time, refer to the transaction involved, and if necessary for his protection, place a condition upon his promise such as the performance of the contract by the other party. If the instrument is negotiable in form, an innocent purchaser may collect it in spite of failure of the consideration for which it was given.

Under the Uniform Negotiable Instruments Law, now adopted in fifty-one jurisdictions, the requirements for a negotiable instrument are laid down as follows:

Sec. 1.—An instrument to be negotiable must conform to the following requirements:

1. It must be in writing and signed by the maker or drawer.

2. Must contain an unconditional promise or order to pay a sum certain in money.

3. Must be payable on demand, or at a fixed or determinable future time.

4. Must be payable to order or to bearer; and

5. Where the instrument is addressed to a drawee, he must be named or otherwise indicated therein with reasonable certainty.

Words of Negotiability.—In order to be negotiable, the instrument must be payable to "the order of A," or to "A's order," or to "bearer," or to "A or bearer." These words of negotiability indicate an intention that the paper shall be transferable. A check payable to a fictitious or non-existing payee (as to cash) is payable to bearer.

Certainty.—No requirement is more fundamental in connection with negotiability than certainty of terms. The promise or obligation of a negotiable instrument cannot be contingent or conditional. It must be certain, both as to the sum to be paid and as to the time of payment.

Certainty as to Amount.—Certainty as to the amount payable is not affected by the following provisions:

Sec. 2.—The sum payable is a sum certain within the meaning of this act, although it is to be paid:

1. With interest; or

2. By stated installments; or

3. By stated installments, with a provision that upon default in payment of any installment or of interest, the whole shall become due; or

4. With exchange, whether at a fixed rate or at the current rate; or

5. With costs of collection or an attorney's fee, in case payment shall not be made at maturity.

When Promise is Unconditional.—By Section 3 of the N. I. L.

Sec. 3.—An unqualified order or promise to pay is unconditional within the meaning of this act, though coupled with:

1. An indication of a particular fund out of which reimbursement is to be made, or a particular account to be debited with the amount; or

2. A statement of the transaction which gives rise to the instrument.

But an order or promise to pay out of a particular fund is not unconditional.

The distinction between an order or promise to pay out of a particular fund, as out of any amount due the drawer on a certain contract or shipment, and an indication of a particular fund, out of which the drawee may reimburse himself, or to which he may debit the amount, is not always easy to determine.

Certainty of Maturity.—Section 4 of the N. I. L. indicates when the time of payment may be considered certain.

Sec. 4.—An instrument is payable at a determinable future time, within the meaning of this act, which is expressed to be payable:

1. At a fixed period after date or sight; or

2. On or before a fixed or determinable future time specified therein; or

3. On or at a fixed period after the occurrence of a specified event which is certain to happen, though the time of happening be uncertain.

An instrument payable upon a contingency is not negotiable, and the happening of the event does not cure the defect.

Additional Terms.—A negotiable instrument must not contain a promise to do anything in addition to the payment of money. By Section 5 of the N. I. L.

Sec. 5.—An instrument which contains an order or prom-ise to do any act in addition to the payment of money is not negotiable. But the negotiable character of an instrument otherwise negotiable is not affected by a provision which:

1. Authorizes the sale of collateral securities in case the instrument be not paid at maturity; or

2. Authorizes a confession of judgment if the instrument be not paid at maturity; or

3. Waives the benefit of any law intended for the advantage or protection of the obligor; or

4. Gives the holder an election to require something to be done in lieu of payment of money.

But nothing in this section shall validate any provision or stipulation otherwise illegal."

Thus a stipulation as follows would not affect the negotiable quality of an instrument: "I have deposited herewith ten $100 Liberty Bonds as collateral security, which I authorize the holder to sell at public or private sale, in case this instrument be not paid at maturity." Forms of authority to appear and confess judgment in favor of the holder of the instrument, if not paid when due, and of waiver of demand and notice of dishonor, will be given below.

Various Matters Which Do Not Affect Negotiability. —By Section 6 of N. I. L.

The validity and negotiable character of an instrument are not affected by the fact that:

1. It is not dated; or

2. Does not specify the value given, or that any value has been given therefor; or

3. Does not specify the place where it is drawn or the place where it is payable; or

4. Bears a seal; or

5. Designates a particular kind of current money in which payment is to be made.

But nothing in this section shall alter or repeal any statute requiring in certain cases the nature of the consideration to be stated in the instrument.

Bearer Paper.—By Section 9 of the N. I. L., the instrument is payable to bearer:

1. When it is expressed to be so payable; or
2. When it is payable to a person named therein or bearer; or
3. When it is payable to the order of a fictitious or non-existing person and such fact was known to the person making it so payable; or
4. When the name of the payee does not purport to be the name of any person; or
5. When the only or last indorsement is an indorsement in blank.

Date and Blanks.—Where the instrument is dated, such date is deemed prima facie to the true date of the making, drawing, acceptance or indorsement, as the case may be. An instrument is not invalid for the reason that it is ante-dated or post-dated, provided that this is not done for an illegal or fraudulent purpose. Where an instrument is issued undated, any holder may insert therein the true date of issue or acceptance. Where an instrument is wanting in any material particular, the person in possession thereof has a prima facie authority to complete it prior to negotiation by filling up the blanks therein.

Every contract on a negotiable instrument is incomplete and revocable until delivery of the instrument for the purpose of giving effect thereto.

Rules of Construction.—By Section 17, N. I. L., Where the language of the instrument is ambiguous, or there are omissons therein, the following rules of construction apply:

1. Where the sum payable is expressed in words and also in figures and there is a discrepancy between the two, the sum denoted by the words is the sum payable; but if the

words are ambiguous or uncertain, references may be had to the figures to fix the amount;

2. Where the instrument provides for the payment of interest, without specifying the date from which interest is to run, the interest runs from the date of the instrument, and if the instrument is undated, from the issue thereof;

3. Where the instrument is not dated, it will be considered to be dated as of the time it was issued;

4. Where there is a conflict between the written and printed provisions of the instrument, the written provisions prevail.

5. Where the instrument is so ambiguous that there is doubt whether it is a bill or note, the holder may treat it as either at his election;

6. Where a signature is so placed upon the instrument that it is not clear in what capacity the person making the same intended to sign, he is to be deemed an indorser;

7. Where an instrument containing the words "I promise to pay" is signed by two or more persons, they are deemed to be jointly and severally liable thereon."

Signature by Agent.—Signature of any party may be made by a duly authorized agent. One who signs in a trade or assumed name will be liable as if he had signed his own name. Where a person adds to a signature words indicating that he signs for or on behalf of a principal, he will not be personally liable on the instrument if he is duly authorized; but the mere addition of words describing him as an agent, without disclosing his principal, does not exempt him from personal liability. Where a signature is forged or made without the authority of the person whose signature it purports to be, it is wholly void and inoperative. A forged check cannot be charged by a bank against a depositor, as the payment to the forger was unauthorized.

Joint Notes.—If it is desired to draw a joint promissory note, the note should read: "We promise." A note which reads "I promise," signed by two or more makers, is a joint and several note. If it is desired to draw a *joint* and *several* note, the note may read: "We jointly and severally promise to pay," proceeding as above, and signed by both makers. It is preferable for the creditor to have a joint and several note, as otherwise in case of suit he will have to sue the makers jointly.

Place of Payment.—It is important to have notes and other negotiable instruments always made payable at a particular place. This is better for the holder, as he can make presentment of the instrument there and demand payment. It is also better for the debtor, as he can make tender and stop interest by having the money at the place where the instrument is made payable. If the debtor goes to that place ready, willing and able to make payment, but the creditor is not there, that is equivalent to tender. If there is no place of payment named, either party may be placed at a disadvantage by having to seek out the other.

Interest.—The payment of interest should be expressly provided for. Unless the instrument says to the contrary, interest will run from the date of the instrument. A post-dated or ante-dated note will get so much the less or more interest. The specified interest will run until the note is paid, whether higher or lower than the legal rate; that is, the contract rate governs not only before maturity but also afterwards. If the note reads "with interest at blank per cent" or with "blank interest," it would probably be held that interest at the legal rate is to be implied in the absence of other agreement. If there is no agreement for interest in the note at all, interest runs from maturity of time paper, and on demand paper runs from delivery.

Compound Interest.—In some States an agreement to pay interest upon interest before the interest has

accrued and become payable, is invalid as being against public policy. (Young v. Hill, 67 N. Y. 162, 23 American Decisions, 99.) Interest on interest is not recoverable in Minnesota unless the contract is in the form of interest coupons as on bonds. In Illinois if the debtor agrees that the annual interest, if not paid, shall become part of the principal and bear interest at the same rate as the original principal, this is held to be a provision for compound interest, which is not recoverable. But interest bearing coupons may be attached to bonds or notes, interest on which is compounded once only and not indefinitely. (Bowman v. Neely, 137 Ill. 433; Telford v. Garrels, 132 Ill. 350; Palm v. Fauchet, 93 Miss. 785, 48 So. 818, 33 L. R. A. (N. S.) 297 note.)

Indorsement.—Indorsement of a negotiable instrument is, (1) a transfer of title to the indorsee so that he can sue in his own name; (2) an implied contract by which the indorser makes himself responsible for payment after due presentment is made and notice of dishonor given. The customary form of indorsement is made by writing the name across the back of the paper. The unqualified indorser engages that on due presentment the instrument will be accepted and paid, and that if dishonored, he will compensate the holder or a subsequent indorser, who is compelled to pay, provided due notice of dishonor is given.

Forms of Indorsement.—(1) A **blank indorsement** specifies no indorsee and consists simply of the signature of the holder, Richard Roe. This makes the instrument payable to bearer. After indorsement in blank, therefore, no further indorsement is necessary, and the instrument will pass by delivery as one payable to bearer. It is dangerous to lose an instrument so indorsed. Any holder may convert a blank indorsement into a special indorsement by writing the name of some payee above the signature.

(2) **Special Indorsement.**—This specifies the person to whom or to whose order the instrument is payable and requires indorsement by him. It is in form simply an order. It may read either "Pay to the order of William Wells, signed by Richard Roe," or "pay to William Wells or order, Richard Roe," or simply "pay to William Wells, Richard Roe." An indorsement does not require words of negotiability such as "to the order of." The effect is the same in all cases.

(3) **Qualified Indorsement, "Without Recourse."**—It is not always understood that an indorsement, although qualified by the words "without recourse," implies a warranty, (a) that the instrument is genuine; (b) that the indorser has a good title; (c) that prior parties had capacity to contract; (d) that he has no knowledge of facts that would impair the validity of the instrument or render it valueless. Such indorser does not guarantee, however, acceptance or payment, or that the instrument is a valid or subsisting obligation, aside from forgery, alteration or incapacity. If there is any forged signature on the paper one who indorses "without recourse" would be liable for damage caused by the forgery.

(4) **Indorsement Without Recourse and Without Warranty.**—An instrument may be indorsed "Without recourse and without warranty, express or implied." Such indorsement would pass title, but would seem to relieve the indorser of all further responsibility.

(5) **Restrictive Indorsement.**—This may prohibit the further negotiation of the instrument or constitute the indorsee merely the agent or trustee of the owner; e. g., "Deposit to my account, Richard Roe." "Pay to the

Bank of Wisconsin for collection, Richard Roe." "Pay
A or order for the benefit of B." In depositing a note,
check or other instrument for collection in another city
it is a wise precaution to indorse it *"for collection."*
This charges correspondent banks with notice of the
rights of the ultimate owner and may prevent loss in
case of insolvency of the initial or collecting bank.

(6) **Indorsement and Waiver.**—"Protest waived," or
"Presentment, demand and notice of protest waived, and
consent to extension of time without notice to me.
Richard Roe." Such waiver dispenses with these implied
conditions to the liability of indorser. (L. R. A. 1916 B.
941, N. I. L. 40, 41.)

If a waiver is contained in the body of the instrument, presumably it applies to all persons who sign or
indorse it; but if it is written above the signature of an
indorser, presumably it applies only to the indorser
whose name is written underneath. But one might
print or write on the back a waiver which would apply
to all, as "all indorsers on this instrument waive notice."

When the holder of a check procures it to be certified by the bank, the drawer and all indorsers are discharged from further liability.

(7) **Name Misspelled.**—Where the name of the holder
is misspelled, as where a check is made payable to
"John A. Brown," where the payee's true name is
"James K. Browne," the instrument should be indorsed
by signing the name by which he is designated in the
check, adding thereunder his correct name if he so desires. (N. I. L. sec. 43.)

Drafts and Bills of Exchange.—A bill of exchange
or draft is an unconditional order in writing by which
A directs B to pay to C or to his order, or to bearer,
a certain sum of money at a fixed or determinable future

time. A check is simply a bill of exchange drawn on a bank, payable on demand. A usual form of draft is as follows:

Chicago, Ill., Nov. 11, 1920.
At sight pay to the order of C, three hundred dollars; value received, and charge same to the account of
To: B   A.

In this draft A is the drawer, B is the drawee, and C the payee. B, the drawee, is not liable unless he accepts the bill and assents to the order of the drawer.

If B accepts the order he writes the word "Accepted" in red ink across the face of the bill and signs his name. It is well to add, also, the date of the acceptance, the date that it is payable and the place. Thereafter B is known as the Acceptor and becomes primarily liable. The document is then known as an accepted bill or *"Acceptance."* If the payee wishes to transfer the paper he indorses it and becomes also responsible as an indorser.

An accepted draft can circulate in the same way as a promissory note of the acceptor. The drawer is liable somewhat after the manner of an indorser. A *"bank acceptance"* is a draft of which the drawee and acceptor is a bank or trust company. A *"trade acceptance"* is a draft drawn by a seller, and accepted by a buyer for the price of goods purchased. The seller may thus obtain a negotiable instrument representing the price of goods sold, which may be discounted by banks. It is "two name" paper, as both the drawer and acceptor are behind it.

A time bill of exchange or trade acceptance, given at the time of the purchase of goods, is an acknowledgment of indebtedness and a promise to pay it at a future date, usually thirty, sixty or ninety days distant. These instruments of credit are intended to pass from hand to hand and to be easily convertible into cash. The course of business often is for the seller to draw on the buyer, who accepts the bill and returns it to the seller, who discounts it with his bankers or with some individual purchaser.

The draft or bill of exchange is a common method of collection from a debtor residing in another city. The payee of a draft is often a bank or express company selected by the drawer to make a collection from a debtor. The draft is sent to the bank by mail to collect and remit the proceeds, less collection charges. It may, of course, be drawn in favor of any one to whom the drawer wishes the money paid by the drawee. There is no obligation upon a drawee to honor or accept a draft, even if he owes the money, and no penalty if he fails to do so.

Banks frequently serve as collection agencies to present drafts for collection which are attached to bills of lading for goods sold. If the draft is discounted by the collecting bank, signatures of the drawer and acceptor of the draft form one part of the security, and the goods another, if an order bill of lading is indorsed with the draft.

Sometimes the bill of lading is turned over to the buyer and the bank retains its lien by a *"trust receipt,"* that the bill of lading, the goods and their proceeds and any part thereof, are to be held by the acceptor in trust, for payment of the draft or debt of the consignee. The receipt may provide: "We hereby engage to hold the said goods in trust, in your behalf, to have them duly stored, insured against fire, and to remit to you the proceeds as and when sold." Unless this provision is stamped upon the bill of lading itself, a purchaser of the bill of lading might take the goods free from the lien of the banker. (Williston, Lectures on Commercial Law, sec. 167.)

Post-dating Checks.—A post-dated check may be made to perform some of the functions of a time bill. The maker may wish to make a payment which falls due at a future date, January 1st, and he may not provide a balance sufficient to meet the check until that time. The bank can only pay the check and debit the depositor's account at the time authorized. Post-dated checks are valid and negotiable instruments (N. I. L., sec. 12; 29 Yale Law Journal 321). Drafts or checks payable otherwise than at sight or on demand require a stamp tax of two cents on each $100 or fraction thereof under the Federal Revenue Act of 1918.

Note—Stamp Tax.—Promissory notes require revenue stamps of two cents for each $100 or fractional part thereof under the Federal Revenue Act of 1918. The expense will usually be borne by the party who furnishes the instrument. Whoever signs, issues or accepts any instrument or document without the full amount of the tax thereon being duly paid is guilty of a misdemeanor and liable to a fine of $100.

Exercises in Bills and Notes.—

(1) Draw a negotiable promissory note in which John Doe promises to pay you $1,000 on January 1st next. Add provisions for compound interest and attorney's fees in legal form if possible.

(2) Draw a note so that the maker can pay it at any time.

(3) Draw a note binding on a corporation of which you are an officer, but which will not bind you.

(4) Draw a note authorizing the holder to obtain judgment by confession against the maker.

(5) Draw a bank acceptance and also a trade acceptance.

Forms of Draft or Bill of Exchange

Chicago, Ill., October 1, 1920.

twenty)

On demand (or at sight, or in   sixty) days after

ninety)

date (sight) pay to the order of Richard Roe, One thousand ($1,000.00) Dollars, for value received, and charge the same to my account. (With interest at .... per cent per annum.)

To: John Smith,   John Doe.

New York City, N. Y.

Note.—If the drawer and payee are the same person the draft may read: "Pay to the order of Ourselves."

An acceptance of this bill would read:

"Accepted. New York, October 3, 1920.

"John Smith."

and would be written across the face of the bill.

Note.—The acceptance may make the draft payable at a particular place or upon the delivery to me of a bill of lading for certain goods or on whatever other condition may be desired—e. g.,

"Accepted, payable at the First National Bank only.

"John Smith."

Or, "Payable July 1, 1920."

By the N. I. L. a draft payable at sight or where no time is expressed, is payable on demand.

Guaranty of Note and Expenses of Collection

"For value received the undersigned jointly and severally indorse and also guarantee the payment of the within note at maturity to any holder, together with interest at the rate of seven per cent per annum until paid, and agree to pay all cost and expenses incurred in collecting the same together with attorney's fees, waiving demand, protest and notice of dishonor and diligence in collection.

Richard Roe,
John Doe.

Assignment of Debt or Chose in Action

"Know all men by these presents:—That I, A. B., for value received, viz.; ...., hereby assign and transfer to C. D. the debt owing to me by X. for (here insert description of debt or claim) and appoint him my attorney with irrevocable power to collect the same for his own use and benefit, with full power to collect and receipt for same, but at his own cost. I guarantee that said debt is due and owing at this date."

A. B.

Form of a Mortgage Note Payable in Installments.— Following is a form of mortgage note from Peter Poor and wife to Samuel Rich for Five Thousand Four Hundred and Fifty Dollars ($5,450.00), dated Sept. 1, 1920, payable in five years in installments of Five Hundred Dollars ($500), on or before Sept. 1st each year, and the balance at the end of five years. Interest at 6% is to be paid quarterly and is to be compounded if not paid when due. There is an *acceleration clause* providing for maturity of the entire note in case of default in payment of interest or installments continuing for a period of thirty days. The makers are to have the privilege of paying off the principal in multiples of Five Hundred Dollars ($500.00) on any interest date.

$5,450. Madison, Wis., Sept. 1, 1920.

FOR VALUE RECEIVED, I promise to pay Samuel Rich, or order, Five Thousand Four Hundred and Fifty Dollars ($5,450.00) in the following manner: Five Hundred Dollars ($500.) on or before Sept. 1, 1921; Five Hundred Dollars ($500.) on or before Sept. 1, 1922; Five Hundred Dollars ($500.) on or before Sept. 1, 1923; Five Hundred Dollars ($500.) on or before Sept. 1, 1924; Three Thousand Four Hundred and Fifty Dollars ($3,450.00) on or before Sept. 1, 1925. The unpaid principal of this note shall bear interest from the date hereof, at the rate of ...... six ...... (6) per cent per annum. Said interest shall be payable quarterly on the first days of December, March, June and September, so long as the said principal sum or any part thereof shall remain unpaid; with interest on any unpaid installments of interest at the same rate from the date the same shall become due. If default shall be made in the payment of principal or interest or of any part thereof, at the time the same shall become due, or in the performance of any of the conditions of the mortgage of even date herewith and collateral hereto, and such default shall continue for a period of thirty days, the whole of said principal and all of the accrued interest shall thereupon become and be forthwith due and payable without notice to us.

Both principal and interest on the note shall be payable at the Bank of Commerce, Madison, Wis.

The makers of this note shall have the privilege of paying off the principal in amounts of $500, or multiples thereof, on any interest date.

Peter Poor.
Mary Poor.

Incorporation of Mortgages into Notes.—Indebtedness secured by mortgage is usually represented by a promissory note, the terms of which are recited in the mortgage deed. It may be well to incorporate in the note, by reference or recital, all those covenants of the mortgagor which will not make the note non-negotiable, in order that a purchaser of the note may take free and clear of possible defences good between the original parties. In some states, acts have been passed that mortgages shall be exempt from defences to the same extent as the negotiable paper which they secure. Some of these covenants, such as the acceleration provisions, may render the note non-negotiable (32 Harv. Law. Rev. 747).

Form of **Note with Acceleration Provision**, and pledge agreement relating to collateral security; in common use in Boston and vicinity.

.............., Mass., ... 19.....

$............

.... months after date, for value received, ... promise to pay to the .... Trust Company, of ...., or order, at the said Trust Company, ... Dollars, having deposited with the said Trust Company as collateral security for the payment of this or any other direct or indirect liability of .... to the said Trust Company, due or to become due, or that may hereafter be contracted, the following described security:

....
....

Should the market value of the security hereby pledged, or which may hereafter be pledged, for this loan depreciate in the opinion of either the President or Treasurer of said Trust Company, ... agree to furnish satisfactory additional security at the demand of the said Trust Company, so that the market value of the security shall always be at least...... per centum more than the amount of this note. And upon .... failing to deposit such additional security when requested, this note shall become due and payable forthwith, anything hereinbefore expressed to the contrary notwithstanding, and the said Trust Company or its assigns may immediately reimburse themselves by the sale of the security as hereinafter authorized. And .... hereby give authority to the said Trust Company or its assigns to sell, assign, and deliver the whole or any part of the said property, also any security substituted therefor or added thereto, with or without notice or advertisement, either at public or private sale, at the option of the said Trust Company or its assigns, on the non-performance of either of the above promises; any balance of the net proceeds of such sale remaining after paying all sums, whether then or thereafter payable, due from .... to the said Trust Company, on account of this note or otherwise, after paying all legal costs and expenses for collection, sale, and delivery, to be returned to......... And it is further agreed that the said Trust Company or its assigns may bid and become purchasers at such sale, and no other purchaser shall be responsible for the application of the purchase money.

In case the undersigned shall be adjudged a bankrupt, or shall file a voluntary petition in bankruptcy, or shall make a general assignment for the benefit of creditors, or in case a petition shall be filed praying that the undersigned be adjudged a bankrupt, this note shall become forthwith due and payable.

....

Due.................

The above note may be rendered non-negotiable by the acceleration provisions. Acceleration Provisions in Time Paper, Z. Chaffee, Jr., 32 Harvard Law Review,

746 (May 1919). See also Z. Chaffee, Cases on Negotiable Instruments, p. 101.

Judgment·Note With Waivers

$........

.,..................... after date we, the makers,
sureties, indorsers, guarantors, and each of us promise
to pay to .... or order, at the First National
Bank of Champaign, ...Dollars, for value
received, with interest at seven per cent per annum
from date until paid, and ten per cent of the principal
hereof additional, as attorney's fees, if placed in the
hands of an attorney for collection.

We severally waive presentment for payment,
notices of dishonor, protest and notice of protest, and
consent that time of payment may be extended without
notice to us.

We appoint any attorney of any court of record
irrevocably to appear in any court of record in term
time or vacation in any State or Territory of the United
States at any time hereafter, to waive the service of
process and to confess a judgment against any of us
in favor of the owner of this note for the principal of
said note and interest due thereon to the day of entry
of said judgment, together with costs, and ten per
cent of the principal and interest due in addition as
attorney's fees.

We consent to immediate execution upon any such
judgment, and release all errors in entering the same,
and the benefit of all exemption laws.

CHAPTER III

PREPARATION OF POWERS OF ATTORNEY

Purpose of Powers of Attorney.—A power of attorney is nothing more than a written declaration that one person, A, is the agent of another, B, with authority to act for him in some business transaction, as to sell or to buy lands, to execute a conveyance, to make leases, or to borrow money and give mortgages. The purpose of making the power of attorney is first, to satisfy the Statute of Frauds which requires written evidence in certain cases; second, to furnish proof of authority so that it may be recorded or so that third parties will feel safe in dealing with the agent; third, to protect the agent and also to warn him and others of the limits of his authority. Formal powers of attorney are usually under seal, especially corporate powers and those given with reference to land matters.

Powers of Attorney May be Broad or Specific.— The authority conferred may be made very specific, covering the very thing that the principal desires done, as of selling a particular piece of land, described in the power at the price and upon the terms therein named. The power may, on the other hand, be made very general indeed, to sell and convey any or all lands or any part thereof in a certain county or state, or wherever situated which the principal may now own or may hereafter acquire, on such terms and conditions as he shall see fit and for such prices as he may think best, including the power to take a mortgage for part of the purchase money and to execute, acknowledge and deliver good and sufficient deeds of conveyance. Such wide powers involve reposing great confidence in the agent, as they place the principal at the mercy of his honesty and discretion.

Written Instruments Conferring Authority Will Be Strictly Construed.—As the Oregon court said in the United States National Bank v. Herron (73 Or. 391; L. R. A. 1916 C. 125), "The power to borrow money or to execute or deliver promissory notes is one of the most important which a principal can confer upon an agent. It is fraught with great possibilities of financial calamity. It is not likely to be implied." The general words and expressions of a power of attorney are restricted by the specific grants of power, and do not confer upon the agent powers to act for the principal generally. There is a great deal of useless verbiage inserted in formal powers of attorneys, as "ratifying and confirming all that the agent may do in the premises," which has no legal effect whatsoever, and the agent will only have power to execute the specific acts expressly mentioned in the power and those incidental thereto.

One Must Inquire Carefully Into the Authority of An Agent.—The burden of proof is on one dealing with an agent through whom he seeks to charge another as principal that the agent acted within the scope of his authority or that the principal ratified the act. When one contracts with another through his agent, or one who purports to be his agent, it is important both to assure one's self that the agent is acting within the scope of the power or authority granted, and also to have the evidence to prove it in case of need.

The scope of authority may be either actual or apparent, but it is not measured by what the agent declares his authority to be but what the principal has actually or ostensibly given him. A man may well refuse to deal with an agent except upon being furnished with an acknowledged power of attorney, either recorded or to be left in his keeping.

The Formalities of Execution.—The authority to execute a deed and convey land should be given by a document or power under seal, and should be duly recorded in order that evidence of the documents upon which the title depends may appear on the public records. In order to be recorded a power of attorney must be executed and acknowledged with all the formalities of a deed of conveyance. In some states power to contract to sell, mortgage or lease lands must be in writing.

Express power to appoint a substitute in place of the agent, to do any act on behalf of the principal, should be included in the power of attorney if the agent is to have this power, as authority cannot otherwise be delegated. It should be made clear in the power of attorney whether it covers "after acquired property." The wife of the principal should join if the agent is to have power to release dower and homestead.

All authority is revoked by death or insanity of the principal, or by notice of revocation, unless the power is "coupled with an interest," i. e., connected with an interest in the property to which the power relates, as a power of sale in a mortgage. On the back of stock certificates there is ordinarily a blank power of attorney to transfer the stock on the books of the company. The power if signed is irrevocable, and belongs to the owner of the stock who holds the certificate.

A Problem in Construction of the Limits on an Agent's Powers.—A party who deals with an agent

acting under written authority is bound at his peril
to advise himself of the limits on the powers of the
agent to bind the principal. A good illustration is furnished by a recent Oregon case in which Mrs. Shehan
gave to Mr. Herron the following Power of Attorney. The question was presented whether two notes
executed by the agent, Herron, one for $3,000 and one
for $2,000 in the following terms were covered by this
power.

Power of Attorney

Know all men by these presents, that I, Catherine L.
Shehan, a widow of Washington City, in the District of Col-
umbia, do hereby make, constitute and appoint Charles E.
Herron, of Vale, in the State of Oregon, my true and lawful
attorney, in and for the purposes hereinafter mentioned, to-
wit: He is hereby authorized and empowered to execute and
sign my name to a negotiable promissory note and deliver the
same to Harry R. Garrett, said note to be dated September 6,
1910, for the sum of five thousand dollars ($5,000), payable to
the order of said Garret on or before one year after its date,
and bearing interest at six (6) per cent per annum, and payable at any bank at Vale, Oregon. And the said Herron is
further authorized to execute in my name a mortgage or deed
of trust, to secure the payment of said note and interest upon
and covering four hundred and eighty (480) acres of land
owned by me in Malheur county, Oregon, that being all the
land owned by me in said county.

In Witness Whereof, I have hereunto set my hand and
seal this 3d day of September, 1910.

Catherine L. Shehan. (Seal)

Signed, sealed and delivered in the presence of us as witnesses:

Alexander H. Galt,
M. A. Ballinger.

The following is a copy of one of said promissory
notes:

$3,000   Vale, Oregon, September 6, 1910.
On or before one year after date, for value received, I
promise to pay to the order of Harry B. Garrett, at the

United States National Bank of Vale, Oregon, the sum of three thousand dollars ($3,000) in gold coin of the United States, at the present standard value, with interest thereon in like gold coin at the rate of 6 per cent. per annum from date until maturity, interest to be paid semi-annually, and if not so paid, the whole sum, principal and interest, to become due and collectable at the option of the holder of this note, and in case suit or action is instituted to collect this note or any part thereof, I promise to pay, in addition to the costs and disbursements provided by statute, an additional 10 per cent. of the amount sued upon for attorneys' fees.

Catherine L. Shehan,
By her attorney-in-fact, Charles E. Herron.
Charles E. Herron.
Estey A. Herron.

Witness
 J. R. Weaver.
 John W. Corson.

The Supreme Court of Oregon held Mrs. Shehan not bound. (United States National Bank v. Herron and Shehan, Appt. 73 Or. 391, 144 Pac. 661, L. R. A. 1915 C. 125, 135n.)

The notes that he executed provide, in the first place, that the principal shall be paid on or before one year from the date of the note; but they require the interest to be paid semi-annually. This is a clear and material departure from the power conferred upon the agent. The note that he was authorized to execute made the interest collectable at the end of the year; but the notes executed by him made the interest collectable at the end of six months............. The agent had no authority to make the interest collectable semi-annually, or to make the principal collectable at the end of six months, at the option of the holders of the notes, if the interest should not be paid semiannually. The agent by making the interest on said notes collectable semiannually, and providing that, if it should not be so paid, the principal should also become due and collectable at the option of the holders thereof, acted outside of the authority conferred upon him and contrary thereto. The notes that he executed, and also the mortgage given to secure their payment, are

not the notes or mortgage of Mrs. Shehan, and they are
void as to her..........................

But we do not find it necessary to decide whether the
execution of the two notes instead of only one, or having said
notes signed by Charles E. Herron and Estey A. Herron as
makers thereof jointly with Mrs. Shehan, was such a departure from the powers vested in said agent as to invalidate
said notes as to Mrs. Shehan.

We hold that the notes executed are not the notes of
Mrs. Shehan, because the interest was made payable semi-
annually, instead of at the end of the year, and the principal
was made collectable at the end of six months, at the option
of the holder thereof, if the interest should not be paid semi-
annually as required by said notes.

This ruling seems unduly strict, but constitutes a
warning that the powers given must be closely pur-
sued and that in drafting powers of attorney great
care must be exercised to give adequate authority to
cover minor variations of method.

Problem. Requisition for Power of Attorney.—The
Adam Bede Company, an Illinois corporation, with its
principal office in Chicago, Ill., owns land in Madison,
Wis., at the southeast corner of State and Murray
Streets. The company wishes to sell one lot 100 ft.
square at this corner if a purchaser can be found.
The price is to be not less than $10,000. Prepare a
power of attorney authorizing John Brown (1) to
make a contract of sale, and (2) to convey the property by warranty deed on the above terms to such
purchaser as he can find, and (3) collect the purchase
price. Let it be properly executed and acknowledged
so that it may be recorded as an instrument of title
with certificate of authority of the Illinois notary
public if necessary. Consider how a corporate deed
or power should be executed to show proper authorization to the officers to execute the instrument on behalf of the company. The deed is to contain build-

ing restrictions for the benefit of an adjoining tract belonging to the company which shall run with the land.

Problem. Requisition for Agency Contract.—Draw a real estate agency contract, by which John Doe, an owner of a house employs Richard Roe, a real estate broker, to find a customer for the property at a certain price for a certain period at an agreed commission. Make it clear whether or not the agent is to have authority to sign a memorandum of a contract of sale by the owner; agent shall agree to exercise due diligence to find a purchaser.

FORM OF POWER OF ATTORNEY TO SELL AND CONVEY LAND GIVEN BY A CORPORATION

KNOW ALL MEN BY THESE PRESENTS, That the Adam Bede Company, a corporation organized and existing under the laws of the State of Illinois, hereby appoints John Brown of Madison, Wisconsin, its agent and attorney in fact, for the following purposes:

(1) To make a contract of sale of the following described property situated in Madison, Dane County, Wisconsin (here insert description);

Upon the following terms and conditions, to wit: (for the purchase price of $10,000, not less than $2,000 to be paid in cash and the balance to be secured by purchase money mortgage or by a land contract reserving title in the vendor;

(2) To execute, sign, seal, deliver and acknowledge a warranty deed in pursuance thereof:

(3) Also to collect and receive the purchase price thereof, give receipts therefor and to take a purchase money mortgage for part of the said purchase money.

The several lots are to be sold and shall be conveyed subject to the following conditions and stipulations for the benefit of the property sold and the adjoining land of the vendor, and the present and future owners, lessees and tenants from time to time of such property, to wit: that no house of less cost than $5,000 shall be erected on any lot purchased; that no stores, or flats or shops, but only private dwelling houses shall be erected thereon. The burden of such covenant shall pass to each successive owner or occupier, but every owner shall be personally liable for breaches occurring only while he remains owner of the land.

With full power and authority to do and perform every act whatever, requisite and necessary to be done in said premises, and with full power of substitution or revocation.[1]

In witness whereof the said Adam Bede Company has hereunto caused its corporate name to be signed by its president, and its corporate seal to be affixed and attested by its secretary this .... day of September, 1920, at Chicago, Illinois.

ADAM BEDE COMPANY   (Seal)

By John Doe, President, and
Richard Roe, Secretary.

Revenue Stamps.—A power of attorney granting authority to do some act for the grantor requires twenty-five cents in revenue stamps under the Federal Revenue Act of 1918. A proxy for voting at a corporation meeting is ten cents.

---

[1]This means, with full power to appoint a substitute in his place and stead to execute any or all of the powers hereby conferred, and to revoke any such appointment from time to time.

CERTIFICATE OF ACKNOWLEDGMENT

State of Illinois ⎱ ss.
County of Cook ⎰

On this ...... day of September, 1920, before me a notary public appeared, John Doe and Richard Roe to me personally known, who being by me duly sworn, did say that they are the president and secretary, respectively, of the Adam Bede Company, a corporation, and did acknowledge that they did sign and seal and execute the said power of attorney in behalf of said corporation by authority of its board of directors and they executed the same as the free act and deed of said corporation.

....

(Seal)   Notary Public.

Note.—When an acknowledgment is taken outside of the state where the land is situated a certificate of the clerk of a court of record is sometimes required that

(1) The notary public or other officer was duly authorized by the laws of the state to take and certify acknowledgments of the execution of deeds of land in said state.

(2) That the signature of the notary is genuine.

(3) That the certificate of acknowledgment is in accordance with the laws of the state.

FORM OF POWER OF ATTORNEY TO SELL, MORTGAGE, LEASE AND CONVEY REAL PROPERTY GENERALLY

I, A. B., do hereby appoint C. D. (if more than one is intended, add after names, "jointly and each of them severally, my attorneys, and") attorney (1) to sell to any person all or any of the lands (add "leases," "mortgages," or otherwise, if in accordance with the fact) belonging to me, which are described or referred to in the Schedule hereunder written. (2) Also to mortgage or otherwise encumber the same re-

spectively, for securing any sum at any rate of interest, or for
any other purpose. (3) Also, to lease all or any such lands
for any term for which I could myself lease or sub-let the
same, not exceeding twenty-one years in possession, at such
rent, or for such other valuable consideration as my said (insert "attorneys or" if more than one) attorney shall deem fit
(here insert anything required in addition or modification).
(4) And for me and in my name or otherwise to sign all
such deeds, transfers and other instruments, and do all such
acts, matters, and things as may be necessary or expedient
for carrying out the powers hereby given, and for recovering
all sums of money that are now or may become due or
owing to me in respect of the premises, and for enforcing or
varying my contracts, covenants or conditions binding upon
any purchaser, lessee, tenant, or occupier of the said lands,
or upon any other person in respect of the same, and recovering and maintaining possession of the said lands, and for
protecting the same from waste, damages, or trespass. (5)
And I hereby declare that this power shall continue in force
until notice of my death or of the revocation of these presents shall have been received by my said attorney (or attorneys).

In witness whereof, I have hereunto subscribed my name,
this .... day of ...., one thousand
nine hundred and ....

                                   A. B. (seal)
Signed in my presence by the said A. B., who is personally
known to me.
E. F.

General Power of Attorney by a Person Leaving the United States for a Limited Period

KNOW ALL MEN BY THESE PRESENTS, I, A. B., of
.............., being about to leave the United States for ....
calendar months, do hereby appoint C. D., of ...., to
be my attorney to act for me, and on my behalf, and in my
name—

1. To draw and sign my name to checks on my account
current with banks and to endorse all checks or other instruments payable to me.
2. To demand, sue for, and receive any money or property

now or hereafter belonging or due to me, and to give good receipts and releases and indemnities in respect thereof; and to prove for such money or property in bankruptcy, liquidation, composition, winding-up or administration proceedings.

3. To let and manage any real personal property which now belongs or hereafter may belong to me, or which may be bought by my attorney, and to receive the rents and to enforce the payment thereof.

4. To settle, compromise, or compound, or submit to arbitration, any accounts, disputes, claims or actions in which I am or may hereafter be concerned.

5. To invest any moneys received by virtue of the powers hereby conferred on my attorney in the purchase of real property, or in stocks, bonds, shares, or debentures of companies, corporations, or public bodies, and to sell or vary such investments.

6. To draw, accept, sign, endorse and negotiate bills of exchange, promissory notes, scrip and other instruments as may be expedient in the conduct of my affairs.

7. To employ and pay a substitute or substitutes to do any of the acts already mentioned.

8. And generally to execute and do all such deeds and things in respect of the premises as my attorney shall think prudent with all the authority that I myself now, or hereafter may, possess.

9. And I declare that my attorney shall not be answerable for the acts or defaults of any substitute, agent, banker or broker, or for any loss not produced by his own willful default.

And I declare that this instrument shall be irrevocable for .... calendar months computed from the date hereof.

In witness, etc.

A. B.

Power to Execute a Particular Deed

TO ALL TO WHOM THESE PRESENTS shall come, greeting:—

WHEREAS, I, A. B., of ...., am about to enter into an agreement between C. D. and E. F. of the one part, and myself of the other part, in relation to (here state shortly the subject of the agreement), and a draft of the deed embodying the said agreement is annexed hereto as a schedule.

NOW THESE PRESENTS WITNESS that I, A. B., hereby appoint X. Y. to be my attorney to execute for me, and in my name, and as my act, the deed to be engrossed from the said draft contained in the schedule hereto.

BUT I AUTHORIZE MY ATTORNEY NEVERTHE-LESS to give his consent on my behalf to any alterations that he may think fit in the draft before its engrossment, provided that such alterations shall not be incompatible with the general purport and object of the agreement as set forth in the draft.

And I declare that this power of attorney shall be irrevocable for .... calendar months computed from the date hereof.

In witness, etc.

A. B.

(Here add the schedule.)

Form for Appointing a Substitute

WHEREAS, A. B., of ...., while in this country executed under his hand and seal a power of attorney dated the .... day of ...., appointing me, C. D., his attorney for him and in his name (recite the terms of the power with the clause giving authority to appoint a substitute).

NOW THESE PRESENTS WITNESS that I, C. D., by virtue of the authority to do so contained in the said power of attorney, do hereby appoint E. F. to be the attorney of the said A. B. for him, and in his name or in my name, to do all or any of the acts set forth in the said power of attorney in the same way and as effectually as the said A. B. or I myself might have done if present, or as if the said E. F. had originally been appointed attorney of A. B. in the place of myself.

And I, C. D., agree to confirm whatever the said E. F. shall do or cause to be done in and about the premises by virtue of these presents.

In witness, etc.

C. D.

(From Mackenzie on Powers of Attorney.)

CHAPTER IV

PREPARATION OF CONTRACTS FOR SALE OF REAL ESTATE

Need of Legal Advice.—It is either extraordinary rashness or ignorance of affairs that prompts so many laymen to sign important contracts for the purchase or sale of valuable real property without legal advice, in childlike reliance on printed forms and the real estate broker. Too often the broker prepares the contract and attends to the signature by both parties, after which the vendor or the purchaser presents the document to his lawyer for advice in performance, when it is too late to correct the mistakes and oversights in preparation. When one considers that the broker is the agent of the seller, one would suppose that the seller's interests would be sufficiently protected. Nevertheless, the anxiety to close the deal and thereby earn the commission overshadows in the broker's mind the importance of accurate detail in the preparation of the contract, and frequently the purchaser is put in a position to gain an advantage over the seller.

Care and Deliberation Needed.—The desire of the parties (to say nothing of the broker), to close the deal quickly and without expense, should not lead them into the dangers of blindly signing a contract or printed blank filled out in the broker's office. The contract is the governing document in the transaction; the delivery of the deed of conveyance of title constitutes merely the carrying out of what the contract prescribes. The preparation of the contract therefor calls for the utmost care

52

and deliberation. Such transactions furnish one of the commonest subjects of litigation. Much trouble and expense might be avoided by advising with the lawyer before signing the contract, instead of afterwards, and by giving proper attention and study to the terms of the contract.

Nature of Title and Its Qualifications.—The form of the deed and the nature of title to be conveyed require particular attention. The printed forms ordinarily call for a warranty deed, with full covenants of title, conveying a merchantable title free and clear of all encumbrances. The vendor may not be in a position to give such a title, or even a merchantable title. The abstract may disclose that the title is defective owing to lack of administration proceedings in a decedent's estate, or to irregularities in some foreclosure or partition sale on account of which it may be necessary to bring suit to quiet title.

If the land contracted to be sold is subject to easements, leases, restrictive covenants as to building or use, or other encumbrances which are not referred to in the contract, the purchaser can object to the title on this ground; and if the defects are not cured in due time can call the contract off. It is, therefore, important to provide in the contract as to whether or not the purchaser is to take the title subject to easements and restrictions contained in prior conveyances.

According to some printed forms of land contracts, the buyer agrees to take the title subject to all building restrictions of record, existing leases, unpaid installments of special assessments, and party wall agreements. *Before the purchaser signs a contract with such a provision,* he should have a search of title made and inform himself specifically what these things are, as he cannot afterward object to them as defects of title.

When preparing or examining a contract on behalf of a purchaser, great care should be exercised to see that the client gets a title which will serve his purposes. If the purchaser desires to acquire the property for the purpose of building an apartment house, a garage, a theater or business building, and the contract refers to covenants and restrictions in prior deeds, an examination of those covenants and restrictions should be made before the contract is signed to ascertain whether the erection of such a building is prohibited.

Description.—The description of the property sold in the contract and also in the deed is of first importance. The seller should make sure that he has not contracted to convey more than he owns. This sometimes happens when the contract is hurriedly drawn in the real estate office with insufficient data at hand. The result may be a rejection of title by the purchaser at the time of completing the contract.

Terms of Payment.—The terms of payment should be stated in a clear and concise manner. If the property is to be conveyed subject to a mortgage, the date and amount of the mortgage should be accurately stated. The purchaser pays a deposit, usually of about 10 per cent of the price, in part payment upon signing the contract, as a guaranty of performance. The time of completion of the contract by delivery of the deed and payment of the purchase price is customarily fixed far enough ahead to allow for an examination of the title.

Recording.—A contract of sale may be recorded by the buyer if he wishes to protect his interest under the contract against subsequent acts of the vendor. On the other hand, it is not desirable for the vendor's protection that the contract be recorded, since if the contract be broken by the purchaser, the recorded contract may create an apparent cloud upon the title. Stringent provisions are therefore sometimes inserted to prevent recording by the purchaser.

Abstract and Examination of Title.—In some localities it is customary for the vendor to agree to furnish an abstract of title; in others the purchaser is expected to have the title searched as well as examined at his own expense. If the vendor is to supply an abstract of title brought down to date this should be expressly provided for. The purchaser should be required to report in writing to the vendor his objections to the title within a limited time, and the vendor should be given a reasonable time to remove any defects found. Under our present recording system no land title may prudently be accepted without laborious examination by a competent attorney. The expense of examining the title usually rests on the purchaser unless otherwise provided. In mortgages, on the other hand, the borrower is usually required to furnish good security without expense to the lender in passing on the title. The seller should agree to convey a good "merchantable title" of record, that is, one free from doubts and defects which would render it unsaleable, such as unreleased dower rights or defective conveyances.

Security for Deferred Payments.—Land is frequently sold on deferred payments, properly secured. This may be done by an installment contract in which the deed is not to be delivered until the last payment. The purchaser is usually given possession upon making a certain cash payment and pays interest on the unpaid balance of the purchase price. Another method is to make the delivery of the deed upon part payment of the price, the balance being secured by a purchase money mortgage back from the purchaser to the vendor. Since a mortgage is not so easily foreclosed as a land contract, this latter method affords greater security to the purchaser and less to the vendor than the contract method. If there is already a mortgage on the premises the purchaser may assume the payment of the mortgage debt as part of the price, instead of requiring the vendor to discharge the mortgage and clear the title. He will then either pay the balance in cash, purchase under contract, or give the vendor a second mortgage to secure its payment.

If the land is not to be sold on credit, and the entire transaction is to be closed up as soon as title can be searched, a very much simpler form of contract will suffice than where the contract relations are to continue over a long period of credit.

The various matters for which provision should be made or considered in land contracts will be specifically indicated in the following forms; some of these may be tabulated for reference as follows:

POINTS TO BE CONSIDERED IN TYPICAL INSTALLMENT LAND CONTRACT

1. Names, description and designation of parties, including wife of vendor. Date.

2. Agreement for sale and purchase. Consideration.

3. Exact description of the land purchased, verified from deed or abstract or survey, showing county and state where located.

4. Price, mode and time of payment; security; payment by certified check on specified bank.

5. Interest on deferred payments, how payable.

6. Vendor to furnish complete merchantable abstract of title to date certified by a reliable abstract company, showing merchantable title, free and clear of all encum-

brances, with certain possible exceptions. You buy the title, not the land.

7. Date of delivery of abstract of title, and time after delivery within which purchaser is to make objections to the abstract or title shown, if any.

8. Provision to enable vendor to rescind the contract if objections to title are made which he is unable to remove within a reasonable time. [English forms.]

9. The deed, warranty or quit-claim; wife of vendor and all necessary parties to join in deed.

10. Title to be conveyed in fee simple absolute; whether subject to rights of way and other easements, leases, liens and building restrictions, if any, affecting the title.

11. Assumption of mortgage by purchaser, to be included in deed.

12. Fixtures, fittings and crops to be included or to be taken at a valuation.

13. Draft of deed to be submitted by vendor. Date of delivery of deed. Deposit in escrow with bank for delivery on completion.

14. Date when possession is to be given.

15. Apportionment of rents, interest on mortgages, taxes and special assessments.

16. Risk of loss and insurance pending completion of the transfer. Loss clause to be immediately attached to policies.

17. Survey to be made, if any.

18. Forfeiture or partial restitution of purchase money and possession on default. Time of essence.

19. Provision against recording.

20. Effect of destruction of buildings by fire or elements.

21. Liquidated damages and attorneys' fees in case of breach by purchaser.

22. Provision that contract shall bind heirs, assigns, administrators and executors.

23. Revenue stamps to be affixed to the deed.

Forfeiture for Delay.—A stipulation that "time is of the essence of this contract" in a sale of real estate, is very important to the vendor. Where such a stipulation is not inserted and the purchaser fails to pay his money promptly at the appointed day, the vendor may not be able to declare the contract forfeited. With such a stipulation the vendor may take advantage of the slightest delay in tendering payment to call the contract off, unless the delay is excused or waived. Without this clause the delay must be wilful, substantial or serious before it is fatal to the purchaser's rights. From the point of view of the purchaser, it would therefore be advantageous to omit this clause, or to insert some qualification of it to prevent unjust forfeiture.

Assumption of Mortgage.—The assumption of a mortgage which is outstanding, will make the purchaser personally liable to the mortgagee. If the premises are sold simply subject to an existing mortgage lien, there will be no obligation on the part of the purchaser to remove the mortgage, but he will be under the necessity of doing so to protect his title. If the purchaser assumes and agrees to pay the mortgage debt, the purchaser makes himself personally liable. The vendor will remain liable to the mortgagee also, but will stand in the position of a surety only. It is often more convenient for the purchaser to assume an existing mortgage than to go to the expense and trouble of paying off the mortgage and having to make a new one to the vendor to secure the balance of the purchase price. It is well if you purchase subject to a mortgage, or if you assume payment of a note and mortgage, to ascertain the exact amount due thereon, to see that all payments of principal and interest are properly indorsed on the note, and that the note is surrendered up at the time of payment and the mortgage released. If you purchase free from incumbrances, the release of any mortgage on the property should be recorded before or at the time that the transfer of the property is completed. Provision as to the assumption of the mortgage debt should be included in the contract and also in the deed of conveyance.

Insurance.—It is important to provide as to the effect of destruction of buildings by fire or the elements since it is the law in most jurisdictions that the risk of loss is on the purchaser. Even if the property was insured by the vendor, if no provision about insurance is inserted in the contract, and the consent of the insurance company to assignment of the policies was not obtained, the purchaser can not call on the vendor to give him the benefit of the insurance or make any deduction from the purchase money on account of the loss. It must be remembered that a policy of fire insurance is a strictly personal contract for the indemnity of the insured. It is not assignable without the consent of the insurance company or its agent. Such consent should be indorsed on the policy by the agent to make it cover the interest of a purchaser or a mortgagee. As soon as the contract is signed a rider should be attached to policies making them payable to the parties as their interest may appear.

Possession.—Provision should be made for the date of the delivery of possession. It may be noted that in the absence of express stipulation no right of possession in the purchaser will, as a general rule, be implied pending completion of the contract, where the contract is silent as to possession. If interest is payable on the entire purchase price, a right of possession may be implied, as interest is balanced against the rents and profits. The effect of failure to deliver possession may be considered.

In view of the housing situation, it is important in preparing contracts for the sale of real property to consider possible difficulty in getting possession. In representing a seller, the contract should state that the sale is to be made subject to existing tenancies. In representing a purchaser who desires possession for himself, the contract should be made expressly conditional on the delivery of possession by a certain date, in view of difficulty and delay that may occur in getting the present tenant out.

Escrow.—It is convenient to provide that the deed shall be executed promptly and placed in escrow ready for delivery on completion of the contract.

Taxes.—Taxes for the current year may be apportioned according to the period for which they are assessed. Taxes often become a lien in the Spring, but are not payable till the next year. If a tax is a lien upon the land at the date of delivery of a deed the grantor is bound to pay it, unless the contract provides that the purchaser shall take subject to the lien.

Reservations.—Where a grantor sells off a portion of his land retaining a part, he should see that rights of way, drainage, light, and prospect are definitely and expressly reserved for his benefit, if needed, as he will impliedly retain no easements over the portion of the land granted, except easements of necessity and mutual and reciprocal easements.

Options.—An option is a right to purchase property for a fixed period of time. It should recite a substantial consideration, as some courts are hostile to real estate options on nominal consideration and will not specifically enforce them. Some printed forms of option do not provide any time for examination of title by the purchaser or for the delivery of any abstract of title by him. An option should contain the essential provisions of a contract for sale, viz., an accurate description, the purchase price, method of acceptance, the terms of payment and the kind of title to be conveyed. It should ordinarily provide for acceptance by written notice on or before a certain date, accompanied by a certain deposit on the purchase price. It may provide for the delivery of an abstract by the seller, a certain time for objections to title by the purchaser, and the date of delivery of a warranty deed and the payment of the balance of the purchase price. A form of option follows.

Form of Option Land Contract[1]

THIS AGREEMENT made this first day of September, 1920, WITNESSETH: That I, A. B. Carter, of Chicago, County of Cook, State of Illinois, in consideration of $10 to me in hand paid by C. D., of Tampico, do grant said C. D., his heirs and assigns, the sole and exclusive option, for the period of one year from date, to purchase the following described parcel of land of which I am the owner, situated in the State of Illinois, County of Whiteside, one mile southwest of Tampico, Illinois, now occupied by John Nelson (add further description).

If the said C. D. shall at any time within one year from the date of this agreement give notice of acceptance in writing and within thirty days thereafter pay the sum of $10,000, I agree upon said payment to convey to the said C. D., or to such person as he may direct the described premises by warranty deed in fee simple, and furnish on his acceptance of this option a merchantable abstract of merchantable title. Fifteen

---

[1]Note.—For forms of Options see III Devlin on Deeds, pp. 3213, 3217, 3252, 2968. See also 185 Ill. 308; 183 Illinois App. 156; 206 Ill. 310.

days are allowed for examination of said abstract and objection to title.

If the said C. D. shall be the cause of any person or persons purchasing the above described property I agree that he shall be entitled to a commission of all over the said purchase price of $10,000.

If before the expiration of this option I fail to notify the said C. D. to the contrary, this option shall be considered to be renewed and extended on the same terms of purchase for one year.

IN WITNESS WHEREOF, I have set my hand and seal.

A. B. Carter   (Seal)

SHORT LAND CONTRACTS

The following is a short form of land contract suitable for parties contemplating early completion:

THIS AGREEMENT, made and entered into at Madison, Wis., this first day of June, 1920, by and between Adam Bede and Mary, his wife, vendors, and Noah Williams, purchaser;

The said vendors hereby agree to sell and convey in fee simple, to the said purchaser, who agrees to purchase for the sum of $20,000, all that parcel of land with the building and appurtenances thereto belonging, situate in the County of Dane, and State of Wisconsin, described as follows: (Homestead, Farm, etc.)

Said premises are sold and purchased for the sum of $20,000, upon the following terms, namely:

1. The purchaser shall pay to the vendor upon the execution of this contract, a deposit of One Thousand Dollars, receipt of which is hereby acknowledged, in part payment of the purchase money, and shall pay the balance thereof by cash or certified check, at the X Bank in Madison in the manner following: (On........ day of ....)

2. The vendors shall within thirty days from the date hereof, furnish and deliver to the said purchaser a full and complete abstract of title to the said premises brought down to date, showing a merchantable title of record. Any objections to the title or to the abstract shall be delivered in writing to the vendors within .... days from the delivery of the abstract, and the vendors shall have ...... days to remove said objections.

3. The vendors, upon the payment by the purchaser of the entire purchase money and concurrently therewith, shall make, execute, acknowledge and deliver a good and sufficient deed of general warranty—conveying a good record title to said premises in fee simple absolute, free and clear of all liens, special assessments, and encumbrances except as follows: (1) Assumption of mortgage.

4. The vendors shall forthwith have the fire insurance policies upon said premises made payable to vendors and purchasers as their interest may appear by consent of the insurance company.

5. The said purchaser will pay all assessments and taxes that may be levied or assessed upon said premises after Aug. 1, 1920.

6. Full possession of said premises is to be delivered to the purchaser at the time of the delivery of the deed, and said premises are to be then in the same condition in which they now are, damage by fire or elements and reasonable use and wear of the buildings thereon only excepted. (Fixtures and fittings to go with premises.)

7. If the said purchaser fails to pay the said purchase money on the very day specified, then this agreement is to become voidable as regards the said vendors, at their option; and whatever may have been paid on this agreement shall be absolutely forfeited. Time is of the essence of this contract. Interest on payments not made when due at seven (7) per cent per annum.

8. The stipulations aforesaid are to apply to and bind the heirs, executors, administrators and assigns of the respective parties.

IN WITNESS WHEREOF, the said parties have hereunto set their hands and seals to this contract in duplicate the day and year first above written.

Adam Bede	(Seal)
Mary Bede	(Seal)
Noah Williams	(Seal)

Signed, sealed and delivered in
the presence of:
   John Doe
   Richard Roe

Requisition for Installment Contract.—Let us now consider a typical case which calls for the drawing of a more elaborate contract for the purchase and sale of a farm under an installment contract.

Adam Bede is the owner of the Homestead Farm of 160 acres in this state on which are situated a farm house, also barns and ou buildings. His wife, Mary, lives with him on the farm which he occupies as a home. Noah Williams wishes to buy the farm, including the house and farm buildings, at the price of $20,000, payable in installments during a period of four years.

On October 1, 1919, Adam Bede, the vendor, has his farm mortgaged to the X bank to secure payment of a note of that date for $3,000, due in three years with interest payable annually at the rate of 6%. This mortgage was duly recorded in Book 60 of mortgages at page 100.

Williams is to purchase the farm, paying the price of $20,000 as above, but is to assume the payment of the mortgage debt which is to be allowed for on the gross price. He is to receive a deed with the usual covenants of title. The deed is to be in such form as to release whatever rights Mary may have in the land, but she is not to be bound by the covenants.

There are crops planted and growing on the farm. The buildings are insured for $5,000 in the Y Fire Insurance Company, loss payable to the mortgagee.

We are called on to prepare a contract of purchase and sale to cover this case.

Installment Contract for the Purchase and Sale of Land

By this contract made this first day of June, 1920, between Adam Bede and Mary, his wife (herein called the Vendors), and Noah Williams (herein called the Purchaser), it is agreed as follows:

1. **Agreement of Purchase and Sale.**—The Vendors shall sell and convey and the Purchaser shall purchase at the gross price of $20,000, the property known as The Homestead Farm, which premises are more particularly described on the page marked "description," and are delineated on the plan or survey hereto annexed.

2. **Price.**—The Purchaser has this day paid to the Vendors the sum of $2,000 as a deposit and in part payment of the purchase money of $20,000. The said deposit of $2,000 shall be placed on deposit with the .... Bank as stakeholder for the signers of this contract to be released and paid over to the Vendor on the approval of the title and deposit of the deed. The balance of said purchase price of $20,000 shall be paid in the manner following by semi-annual installments, with interest on the unpaid balance of the purchase price at 6 per cent, payable semi-annually:

January 1, 1921	$2,000
June 1, 1921	2,000
January 1, 1922	2,000
June 1, 1922	2,000
January 1, 1923	2,000
June 1, 1923	2,000
January 1, 1924	2,000
June 1, 1924	1,000
Total	$15,000

Payment may be made by certified check on a solvent national bank in the said city or state.

Additional payment in multiples of $100 may be made at the time regular installments are due.

The Purchaser also agrees as part of the price to assume the mortgage debt of $3,000, evidenced by a note and mortgage on the premises herein described made October 1, 1919, by the Vendors to the X Bank, and recorded in Book 60 of Mortgages at page 100. The Purchaser shall indemnify and save harmless the Vendors from liability on said note and mortgage, and if the same is not paid or renewed at maturity, this shall have the same effect as a default in the payment of the purchase price.

3. **Option to Pay Up Entire Balance.**—The Purchaser may at any time on giving seven days' notice in writing, pay off the entire balance of the purchase money remaining due, together with interest thereon to the date of payment, and demand a deed.

4. **Examination of Title.**—The Purchaser shall within 30 days after the date of this contract examine the title to the said premises at his own cost,[2] and shall send to the Vendors a statement in writing of all valid objections to the title, and subject thereto the title shall be deemed accepted, and all objections not included in any statement sent within the time aforesaid shall be deemed waived.

The Vendors shall have 15 days from the receipt of said statement of objections to remove or cure any defects in title which destroy its marketability.

---

[2] If the Vendor already has an abstract of title, he may agree to deliver it to the Purchaser forthwith for continuation to date; or he may in any case agree to procure and deliver to the Purchaser a complete merchantable abstract of title down to date of completion at his own expense. This is a matter for negotiation.

If the Purchaser shall make any objection which the Vendors are unable, or on the ground of expense, unwilling to remove, and the Purchaser shall not waive the objection within ten days after being required to do so, the Vendors may by notice in writing delivered or mailed to the Purchaser, rescind this contract upon repaying to the purchaser his deposit money, and the Purchaser shall not make any claim on the Vendors for damages, costs or expenses.[3]

5. **Possession and Expenses.**—Upon the signing of this contract and payment of the deposit of $2,000, the Purchaser shall be let into possession of the said premises, and enjoyment of the rents, issues and profits thereof, and shall pay all rents, taxes, insurance and other expenses incident to the land from that day; and all rents and taxes shall be apportioned as of that day. In default of the Purchaser paying taxes or insurance the Vendors may pay the same, and add them to the purchase price, according to the period which they are intended to cover.[4]

6. **Interest.**—The unpaid balance of the purchase money shall bear interest at 6 per cent per annum from the date of this contract (or the taking possession) until paid, and said interest shall be payable (quarterly, semi-annually, or annually) as part of the purchase price, and if not paid when due shall be added to the principal and bear interest at 7 per cent until paid.

7. **Use.**—The Purchaser agrees to occupy and culti-

---

[3] It may be provided that if the purchaser within 5 days after receiving the notice to rescind withdraws his objection, the notice to rescind shall be withdrawn also.

[4] It may be provided that the purchaser shall hold possession of said premises as tenant at will of the seller, and subject to be removed as such whenever default shall be made in payment of any of the installments of the purchase price upon ten days' notice.

vate said premises in a careful and husbandlike manner, without committing waste or permitting any nuisance thereon. He shall keep the buildings, fences and improvements on said land in as good repair and condition as the same now are, except for ordinary wear and tear, and unusual damage by the elements.[5]

8. **Insurance.**—The Purchaser shall keep the buildings on said premises insured against loss or damage by fire in the sum of $5,000 in fire insurance companies satisfactory to the Vendors, loss payable to the mortgagee, the Vendors and the Purchaser as their interests may appear.

In case of loss the insurance money shall be expended by and under the direction of the Vendors in the restoration of the improvements damaged. The policies shall be deposited with the Vendors.

9. **The Deed.**—The Vendors hereby agree that after the aforesaid price of $20,000 shall be fully paid at the time and in the manner above specified that they will on demand thereafter execute and deliver to the said buyer, his heirs and assigns, a good and sufficient warranty deed, with full covenants of warranty but not by Mary Bede, conveying said premises above described in fee simple, free and clear of dower and homestead and of all liens and encumbrances, except the taxes agreed to be paid by the Purchaser and excepting and reserving a right of way and of drainage as follows: (here may be given a description of a right of way with or without gates.) The deed to the Purchaser shall be prepared by the Vendors forthwith, and shall be deposited in escrow at the X Bank.

(A draft of the proposed conveyance shall five days

---

[5] It may be provided that the purchaser shall not assign this contract, or lease said property or abandon or part with the possession thereof without the consent in writing of the Vendor.

before the date fixed for completion be furnished for perusal by the Purchaser and final payment shall not fall due until five days after such draft is submitted.)

It is agreed that the title and covenants shall be subject to the following qualifications: (1) all taxes and special assessments levied after .... date, (2) all installments falling due after ...... of special assessments heretofore levied, (3) party walls and party wall agreements if any, (4) building lines and building restrictions if any, (5) the rights of the public in any portion of the premises which may fall within any public street, alley or way.

10. **Forfeiture on Default.**—If the Purchaser shall neglect or fail to perform the contract on his part, the Vendors may declare the contract forfeited upon ten days' notice and upon tendering a deed to the defaulting purchaser (or may resell the premises at auction or by private contract). Prompt payment of the installments of the purchase price and interest and strict performance of all covenants and conditions on the part of the Purchaser are conditions precedent to his right to a deed. Time shall be of the essence of this contract. In case this contract is declared forfeited by the Vendors, the Purchaser shall forfeit all payments made by him on this contract, and all such payments shall be retained by the Vendors as liquidated damages (or $500 or other agreed amount may be retained as such). A written notice of such forfeiture served upon the Purchaser or his successor, or any occupant of the premises, or recorded in the recorder's office of said county, shall be sufficient evidence of such forfeiture.

11. **Fixtures and Fittings.**—The Purchaser is to take the following fixtures and fittings; gas stoves, gas hot water heaters, kitchen range, coal and wood on hand, loose parts of machines; also the threshing machines

and reaping machines, all implements of agriculture, all crops now growing, and all hay, straw and manure at a price to be ascertained by Mr. X; and in case of his failure to value, at the market price. Screen windows and doors, storm windows and doors, window shades, steam, gas and electric light fixtures shall pass as part of the premises.

12. This contract shall extend to and be binding upon the heirs, executors and assigns of the parties hereunto.

IN WITNESS WHEREOF the parties have hereunto set their hands and seals the day and year first above written.

Adam Bede   (Seal)

Mary Bede   (Seal)

Noah Williams   (Seal)

Clause for Purchase Money Mortgage.—Where the balance of the purchase price is to be secured by a first or second mortgage to be given by the purchaser to the vendor on the delivery of the deed it is necessary that the form of the mortgage be settled or arranged for. It is important to provide that the note and mortgage be prepared by the vendor's attorney in form approved by him and at the purchaser's expense; and that the purchaser pay the necessary recording fees and revenue stamps for "the borrower is the slave of the lender." A clause may be included in the contract somewhat as follows: Upon tender of a deed by the vendor the purchaser and his wife will duly execute and sign a negotiable note and mortgage upon said premises for the balance of the price to be drawn up by the vendor containing the usual provisions including covenants for payment of insurance, taxes and assessments until the purchase money is fully paid, with interest on the unpaid balance of the purchase price at the rate of 7 per cent per annum by half yearly payments from the date of the mortgage, the principal sum to be due in three years from the date thereof. Said mortgage shall contain all usual and proper powers and provisions; and if the parties cannot agree on the wording of said mortgage or note, the same shall be settled by the vendor's attorney, whose approval shall be binding upon the parties. The said mortgage is to be acknowledged and recorded at the expense of the purchaser, and the purchaser shall bear all expenses in the preparing and recording of said mortgage.

CHAPTER V

PREPARATION OF DEEDS OF CONVEYANCE

Essentials.—Deeds should be prepared only by a competent conveyancer and should be recorded immediately by the grantee. A deed may be expressed in few and simple words. The essentials of a valid deed of conveyance are a grantor and grantee, a recital of consideration, an expression of an intent to grant or convey, and a description of the property and interest therein conveyed. Such an instrument signed, sealed and delivered would be a valid conveyance. (Kelly v. Parker, 181 Ill. 49, 59.) It is not necessary, though it is prudent, to follow the set forms. The following would suffice to pass title in most states:

This deed is made this first day of June, 1920, between A and B, his wife, of Chicago, grantors, and C, purchaser; in consideration of $10.00 paid by C to A, the grantors hereby convey and warrant to C, his heirs and assigns forever, all that parcel of real property, situated in the town of X, County of Y, and State of Z, which premises are more particularly described as follows:

(Insert full and accurate description of the land.)

      (Signed)   A. and B.   (Seal)

(Add acknowledgment by grantors.)

Formal Parts.—Statutory forms of deed like the above Illinois form are provided in many states, which aim to shorten and simplify conveyances, but the older forms are usually followed. The formal parts of the customary deed of conveyance are as follows:

1. Introduction, giving date of making, names and description of the parties, and their designation in the instrument as grantors, parties of the first part, etc.

2. Recitals showing the purpose or circumstances of the transaction, such as the estate of the grantors when the property belongs to several persons or is subject to mortgage.

3. Recital of the receipt of consideration by the grantor.

4. Granting clause: operative words of conveyance and limitation, by which the transfer of title is declared and the estate or interest conveyed is defined. (Grant or convey is sufficient.)

5. Description of the property conveyed and easements created.

6. General words as to appurtenances, fixtures, etc.

7. Exceptions of any parts of the general tract described which are not to be included.

8. *Habendum* (to have and to hold to the use of said grantee and his heirs), which defines the estate granted, usually a repetition. The word "heirs" should be used to pass a fee. Words of limitation in the granting clause will govern the habendum. Incumbrances to which the title is subject may be stated here, and also declarations of use and trust.

9. Reservations, by which the grantors reserve rights-of-way, drains, and other easements out of the thing granted.

10. Conditions and restrictions as to use, which may provide for forfeiture of the estate and re-entry by the grantor in certain events.

11. Covenants of title, by which grantors insure the grantees against loss by defects or failure of title.

12. Qualifications; such as building restrictions, special assessments, tax liens, or mortgages to which

the title and covenants are subject. Assumption of mortgage by grantee.

13. Conclusion which contains the signature and seals of the grantors.

14. The attestation.

15. Certificate of acknowledgment by notary public is usually necessary for recording purposes.

Introduction.—The two common forms of commencement of a deed are those of the deed poll and the indenture. The deed poll is a form which may be used when the persons executing it are all of one part, i. e., where the grantors only sign. A *deed poll* commences with a formula as follows:

"KNOW ALL MEN BY THESE PRESENTS, that the C. B. & Q. R. R. Co., a corporation created and existing under the laws of the State of Illinois, for and in consideration of the sum of $10.00 to it paid, etc."

The more common and convenient form for deeds is that of the *Indenture,* which purports to be the act of two or more sets of parties:

"THIS INDENTURE, Made this first day of January, 1920, by and between A and B, his wife, of the City of X, parties of the first part, and C, of the City of Y, party of the second part, witnesseth:"

The party who conveys is usually named first as grantor or party of the first part, and the party to whom the deed is made is named as grantee, or party of the second part.

If the grantor is a single man or woman, that fact should be recited, e. g., "a single man," or a "widower." When a woman acquires land and subsequently marries, she may be described with her own first Christian name and her husband's surname, followed by a recital of her former name, as "Mary Bede, formerly Mary Adams."

A person may take a future estate by remainder or use without being named as a party to the deed. If a wife or other person signs and acknowledges a deed but is not named in the commencement or body of the deed as a granting party, it is doubtful in some states whether the interest of such person will pass by the deed and whether it will bar dower. Even if possession is delivered under a deed which the wife does not sign, the statute of limitations will not run against her dower, until after the death of her husband. All persons having any interest in the premises, such as husband or wife, should be made parties to the deed and should sign and acknowledge it.

Date.—It is proper to date deeds as of the day of delivery, as they go into effect on delivery. Frequently, however, they are dated at an earlier day on which other papers relating to the same property were executed. The date of a deed should preferably be be written out in words.

Recitals.—In ordinary cases there is no necessity for recitals. They may be useful to explain the purpose, the title and interest of the parties, or the nature of the property that is to be conveyed, and to assist in showing what is intended to be accomplished by the deed. Such recitals produce an estoppel between the parties to the deed and they cannot set up the contrary of what is so recited. It may be convenient to recite the last conveyance by which the parties acquired title, with reference to the records, as this facilitates identification of the property and search of title. All unnecessary, temporary or doubtful matter, such as reference to contracts, should, in general, be kept out of the deed and so off the public records. It is inexpedient to recite the contract under which the deed is made, as this will make it necessary to record it and to consider its provisions in passing upon the title. [Dart, Vendors and Purchasers (7th Ed.) Chap. 11, p. 5503.]

Consideration.—The deed should always recite the receipt of valuable consideration. The recital of the receipt of some consideration is probably not necessary in most states, but is extremely advisable even in case of deeds of gift. It is worse than useless to recite a consideration of "love and affection," although relationship may be an operative consideration. The nature and amount of the consideration need not be truly stated; a nominal sum, like $10.00 is usually recited, as the purchaser does not wish the price paid to be a matter of public record. The grantors will not be permitted to attack the conveyance by contradicting the recital that some consideration passed; but the parties will not be precluded from showing that the true consideration was different from that recited if the price has not in fact been paid. Frequently in deeds there is added to the recital of a nominal money consideration, such as $10.00, the phrase, "and other good and valuable considerations." This addition is entirely useless.

Words of Grant and Limitation.—It is not necessary to use several words of conveyance in the granting clause, e. g., that said A, "has granted, bargained, sold and conveyed, and does by these presents, grant, bargain, sell and convey to the said B?" Any word or words showing an intent to convey such as grant, bargain and sell, are sufficient. It is absurd to pile up synonyms or to repeat the same verbs in the past and present tense, "as have granted, bargained, sold and conveyed, and do by these presents grant, bargain, sell and convey." The estate or interest granted, "limited" or conveyed should be indicated in the granting clause, as "to B and his heirs forever," "to B for his life," "to B, and C as their heirs to hold as joint tenants in equal shares, and not as tenants in common."

Description.—Perhaps three-fourths of the defects in land titles arise from mistakes and carelessness in description. No pains should be spared to compare and re-compare the description in the deed with a correct description in the abstract of title or with a surveyor's plat and description. The description is usually copied from the last conveyance, as far as possible, or so connected with it as to preserve evidence of the identity of the property.

Boundaries.—Nothing passes by a deed except what is sufficiently described in it, and what is appurtenant or incidental to that which is so described. If the description be too indefinite or vague to locate the boundaries, the conveyance is null and void. Great attention should be given to the exact starting point of the description which should also be made the terminal point. The point of intersection of two streets is the point of intersection of their center lines. Land is usually described by specific boundary lines, such as roads, streets, rivers and monuments, or by courses and distances. These lines are frequently supplemented by reference to descriptive proper names, such as "the Norris ranch," and by reference to lots and blocks on recorded maps and plats. Calls for specific boundaries and fixed monuments control courses and distances; and fixed monuments (as a tree on the bank of a creek) control courses and distances, as being more certain and material. Quantity is never allowed to control courses and distances, but may help where boundaries are doubtful; quantity alone is never sufficient, as "part of a lot, or one acre of a lot." Boundaries upon a stream are flexible and shift with gradual and imperceptible changes of the channel.

Appurtenances.—All easements and rights appurtenant pass with a grant of land as an incident thereto whether mentioned in the deed or not, and the formal clause numerating such incidents in deeds is mere verbiage. All fixtures, buildings and improvements on land will pass in a deed of the land without specific mention. If there are any fixtures or appurtenances as to which there is some doubt, they should be specified and either included or excluded.

Exceptions and Reservations.—If the grantor wishes to subtract or except a part of the land which in general terms he purports to convey, the exception should be inserted after the description of the land granted. The distinction between exceptions and reservations is no longer important. A reservation of the right to cut timber or to extract minerals or a right-of-way for passage should be made in favor of the grantor *and his heirs*. It may follow the description or the *habendum*. It is doubtful how far a reservation may operate to give rights to a third person not a party to the deed.

Habendum.—The *habendum*, that is, the clause that the grantee is "to have and to hold the premises to the use of himself and his heirs forever" is now little more than form, as the estate or interest granted by the deed is usually indicated in the granting clause. If the granting part of the deed contains proper words to limit or define the estate or interest granted an *habendum* may be dispensed with. If there is a direct conflict between the granting clause and the *habendum*, the granting clause will govern. (Morton v. Babb, 251 Ill. 488.) Where the title is conveyed subject to certain encumbrances, such as a mortgage, a lease or a building restriction, this may be stated following the *habendum*.

The *habendum* clause may be used to declare a trust, grant estates in remainder, or to fix the length of leases.

Conditions and Covenants.—Covenants and conditions are frequently inserted in deeds to preserve the value and character of a residence district against cheap buildings and annoying business. Unless these restrictive covenants are made conditions subsequent, their violation does not work a forfeiture of estate. They may in proper cases be enforced by injunction not only as between the original contracting parties, but also by or against their successors in interest. (Van Sant v. Rose, 260 Ill. 401.)

Conditions precedent require something to happen or be fulfilled before the estate can vest, e. g., the death of the grantor. A deed upon condition subsequent conveys the estate subject to be divested and defeated in the event of some contingency, performance or default, e. g., "provided always, that if the mortgagor shall pay the mortgagee One Thousand Dollars ($1,000.00) upon such a day, the whole estate granted shall determine"; and the like. The law does not favor forfeitures, and in case of breach the estate continues, until actual entry made by the grantor to claim the forfeiture.

Warranty and Quit-Claim Deeds.—A warranty deed derives its name from certain personal covenants of title, which impose upon the grantor the duty to insure or indemnify the grantee against loss by failure of title to the extent of the purchase price. The operative words of conveyance generally employed are "grant, bargain and sell," or "convey and warrant," and these words may by statute imply the usual covenants.

A quit-claim deed is not merely a release, but an original conveyance in American law, as effectual for transferring the title to real property as a warranty deed. The only differences between a quit-claim and a warranty deed are in the granting clause, where the words "remise, release, and forever quit claim" are generally employed, and in the matter of covenants. A quit-claim either contains no covenants at all, or only the covenant of non-claim by the grantor, in which case it is sometimes called a special warranty deed or deed of non-claim. The quit-claim is equally effective to divest and transfer "all the right, title, and interest" as a warranty deed, but it will not usually operate to carry a subsequently acquired title like a warranty deed. There is some conflict in the law as to whether the purchaser does not take the risk of title and whether he may be considered a bona fide purchaser for value, taking free and clear from outstanding equities against the grantor under the recording laws. But to the extent that the seller has an interest in the land, quit-claim deeds divest him of it and vest it in the purchaser. The purchaser of land takes the title at his own risk, if he does not insure himself by covenants guaranteeing the title. Under a quit-claim deed, he will have no remedy against his grantor to recover his purchase money if he is later evicted by paramount title, or the land is found to be burdened with liens or encumbrances, in the absence of fraud. Covenants should be qualified where land is sold subject to building restrictions or liens. The grantee frequently assumes and agrees to pay a mortgage on the premises.

The usual covenants of title are:

(1) Of seisin, that the grantor is lawfully seized in fee simple as owner of the premises.

(2) Of right to convey, that he has a good right to convey the same.

(3) For quiet enjoyment, that he will defend the grantee, his heirs and assigns in the quiet enjoyment

and possession of the premises against eviction by any superior title.

(4) Against encumbrances, that the premises are free and clear from any lien or encumbrance.

(5) Of general warranty, that the grantor and his personal representatives will forever warrant and defend the title and possession thereof in the grantee, his heirs and assigns, against all lawful claims whatsoever, except, etc.

(6) Of further assurance, for further assurance or conveyance to perfect the title, if necessary. (3 Devlin Deeds, p. 2859.)

The Conclusion and Execution.—The conclusion mentions the date of the deed, either expressly or by reference to the day and year recited in the premises; as, "In Witness Whereof, the parties have hereunto set their hands and seals on the day and year first above written."

A. B.   (Seals)

The execution of a deed comprises those acts necessary to put the instrument into legal effect and operation, viz., signing, sealing, and delivering, and in some few states attestation by witnesses. Execution by the purchaser is unnecessary, although it is advisable if the deed contains covenants by him.

The statutes of the particular state where the land is situated should be consulted as to the formalities of execution, seals, attestation, and the methods of release of the wife's dower, the husband's curtesy, the waiver or release of the wife's homestead rights, the form of certificate of acknowledgment, and the certificate to the authority of the notary if the acknowledgment is taken out of the state.

The requirement of subscribing witnesses to a conveyance, if any, is purely statutory and is usually only a prerequisite to recording, not to the validity of the conveyance.

Acknowledgment of execution of the deed by all the grantors properly *certified* by some notary public or other official under his seat, is usually a prerequisite to recording, although not so in Illinois. The purpose of acknowledgment of execution by the party is to prove the genuineness of the deed and prevent imposters from recording forged deeds. The certificate of acknowledgment by the officer should never be made by one who is interested in the transaction, as he is disqualified; e. g., a shareholder in the corporation to which the deed is made. (Devlin Deeds, Ch. XIX.) Acknowledgments are frequently taken by notaries over the telephone, but while this may be convenient it is of very doubtful propriety. If the certificate is not in proper statutory form the recording of the deed may not operate as constructive notice. When a deed is executed and acknowledged in another state, the local statutes sometimes require a certificate of the authority of the notary or other officer taking the acknowledgment by the clerk of a court of record. Even if a deed be neither acknowledged nor recorded it will be good as between the parties and subsequent purchasers with actual notice, except in some states as to homesteads. (Roane v. Baker, 120 Ill. 308; Ogden Building & Loan Ass'n v. Mensch, 196 Ill. 554, 569.)

Delivery of the deed completes the conveyance. A deed takes effect only from its delivery, either by the grantor or his agent. The delivery is an essential part of the execution. The instrument may be signed and acknowledged, but as long as the document remains undelivered it is inoperative. Once delivered to the grantee, or to a third person for him, it will be effectual although delivered back to the grantor for custody. Re-delivery for cancellation and destruction may, however, cause insuperable difficulties in proof and amount to a re-conveyance. (2 Wigmore, Evidence, Sec. 1198; 2 Jones, Real Property, Sec. 1259.)

The delivery need not be an actual handing over of the deed to the grantee; a delivery to a stranger for the grantee, or any words or gestures expressing the intent to deliver will be sufficient, although the grantor keeps the instrument in his custody.

Dower is usually barred by having the wife join in the conveyance. In Illinois and some other states, in order to convey the *homestead* it is necessary for the husband and wife to join in the deed which should contain a clause expressly waiving and releasing all rights by virtue of the Homestead Exemption Laws. The certificate of acknowledgment should also contain a recital of the release of homestead, even though the conveyance is to the wife herself.

Recording.—Deeds, mortgages and other conveyances must be promptly recorded in order to give protection and security to the purchaser. Putting the deed on record is the concern of the grantee to protect him against subsequent acts of the grantor and his creditors. Every conveyance not so recorded is void as against any subsequent purchaser without notice in good faith and for value from the grantor who remains the owner of record. Records serve for the preservation of the documents of title, and for notice to all future purchasers of the land.

Alterations.—Neither the notary public nor the grantee may after an instrument is executed change or correct the description of the premises conveyed, or otherwise alter the document without the assent of the grantor, even to make it conform to the intention of the

parties. The erasure, for example, of the grantee's name
and the substitution of another name after final delivery
of a deed without the grantor's consent, would have no
effect upon the title. If the grantee's name in a deed
be left blank and be inserted after delivery in the absence of the grantor and without his authority in writing, the deed would be void in many states, unless the
parties signing and sealing the deed afterwards ratify,
adopt or deliver it. (Osby v. Reynolds, 260 Ill. 576,
581; Mickey v. Barton, 194 Ill. 446, 455.)

Joint Tenancy and Tenancy in Common.—If two or
more persons are named as grantees, they will ordinarily take as tenants in common in equal shares, unless
something to the contrary is stated. In order to create
joint tenancy with the right of survivorship, it is necessary under modern statutes expressly to state that the
grantees shall take "as joint tenants and not as tenants
in common." It is often convenient for husband and
wife to take title to property as joint tenants, as the
right of survivorship avoids the necessity of probate.
In some states where a deed runs to husband and wife,
they take as *tenants by* the *entirety,* a peculiar species
of tenancy.

Conveyance to Partners.—Deeds to partners should
name them individually as grantees, and not simply by
the firm name. The deed may be made to the partners
as joint tenants, and not as tenants in common, in trust
for partnership purposes. Under the Uniform Partnership Act, Section 8, an estate in real property may be
acquired and conveyed in the partnership name.

Deeds to Take Effect at Death.—A grantor cannot
make a deed and leave it among his papers to be delivered after his death, but he may make a deed and deliver it in his lifetime to *some third party,* to be handed

over to the grantee after his death. Such deed must
be put entirely beyond the grantor's control, with no
right of recall or revocation. (See Ballantine, When
Are Deeds Testamentary? 18 Mich. Law. Rev. 470.)

In most states there is no valid delivery if the
grantor delivers a deed to a third party to become
effective only on the happening of some *uncertain* future
event, such as the non-recovery of the grantor from a
particular illness, or the survivorship of the grantee. It
is generally held that such a delivery is ineffectual even
though the condition be fulfilled. (See Ballantine, Delivery in Escrow, 29 Yale Law Journal 826.)

A deed may be made and delivered to the grantee
direct, which by its terms is only to transfer title at
the grantor's decease. Probably the safest method is
for the grantor by express terms to retain or reserve a
life estate without impeachment of waste, and with
power to cut timber and mine coal and oil and mortgage the fee. Deeds containing the usual granting
clause and covenants were sustained as valid instruments of conveyance notwithstanding the following
words were used in the habendum:

"This deed not to take effect until after my decease, not to be recorded until after my decease."
(Shackelton v. Sebree, 86 Ill. 616. Hudson v. Hudson,
287 Ill. 286.)

"To be in force from and after my decease, and
not before." (Latimer v. Latimer, 174 Ill. 418, 51
N. E. 548.)

"This deed shall take and be in full force and effect
immediately after the said William Logan shall depart
this life, and not sooner." Lauck v. Logan, 45 W. Va.
251, 31 S. E. 986. (The court in this case held that
the intention of grantor was to reserve a life estate.)

"To be of no effect until after death of grantor,

and then to be in full force." Wilson v. Carrico, 140 Ind. 533, 40 N. E. 50, 49 Am. St. Rep. 213. Bullard v. Suedemeier, 291 Ill. 400.

"Not to take effect during my lifetime, and to take effect and be in force * * * after my decease." Wyman v. Brown, 50 Me. 139. Bradley v. Bradley, (Iowa) 171 N. W. 729.

On the other hand similar language has been held testamentary in some cases. (See the author, "When Are Deeds Testamentary?" 18 Mich. Law Rev. 470, April, 1920.)

A form of a deed to convey the freehold in futuro might be drafted somewhat as follows:

"This deed conveys a future estate in fee to take effect in possession after the death of the grantor. The title to such future estate shall pass at once, but the grantor reserves a life estate without impeachment of waste. This deed is not subject to revocation, and has been fully delivered."

How to Create Joint Tenancy With Wife by Single Deed.—Joint tenants must take title by the same conveyance. Under the Statute of Uses a man may by a single deed of bargain and sale convey his land to himself in joint tenancy with his wife. This is effected by conveying to the wife or to a third person to the use of B. & C., the persons intended to take jointly. Previous to the statute, in consequence of the rule that a man cannot take an estate by his own conveyance (i. e., unite the characters of grantor and grantee) two conveyances would have been necessary: (1) to a third person; (2) by the third person to him and his wife as joint tenants. (Goodeve R. P., 256; 2 Davidson Prec., Part I, pp. 182, 184.) A. may now convey land to himself jointly with another; A. to B. to the use of A. and B. and their heirs as joint tenants and not as tenants in common; and a joint estate in fee simple will immediately vest in both, with the right of survivorship, which obviates the need of probate or administration by the survivor.

PRACTICAL SUGGESTIONS

1. It would be a prudent practise to have the grantor make formal delivery of a deed in the presence of two or more witnesses, declaring his intent to deliver, and to have the fact attested by the witnesses upon the deed.

2. All necessary corrections in a deed or other instrument should be made before execution or delivery, and should be initialled immediately by the parties and witnesses. It would be better to re-draft the instrument entirely.

3. It may happen that B, having agreed to purchase a house or lot of A for $5,000, has agreed, in his turn, to sell it to C for $6,000 before he has completed his purchase. In such a case there is no need for A to convey to B and then for B to convey to C, but the transaction may be carried out by one deed from A and B to C. A may be made party of the first part, B of the second part, and C of the third part. The original contract of sale to B and the sub-sale to C may be recited. The expense of drawing and recording two separate deeds is thus avoided.

4. Deeds by corporations should be made by their officers properly authorized for the purpose. It is well to have a certified copy of the vote or by-law authorizing the execution of the deed.

5. Deeds executed by an agent should be accompanied by the original power of attorney duly executed and acknowledged for recording.

6. Deeds conveying real estate, except mortgages

and instruments given to secure a debt, require revenue stamps, under Federal Revenue Act of 1918, of 50 cents per hundred dollars of consideration, exclusive of encumbrances assumed.

PROBLEMS AND EXERCISES

1. Draw a warranty deed from John Doe and wife to Richard Roe and his wife as joint tenants, subject to a mortgage which the grantees assume.

2. Draw a deed to the assignee of the purchaser under a land contract, the original purchaser joining with the vendor in the deed.

3. Draw a form of deed of coal mining rights which shall not include the surface or surface rights except so far as necessary to mine the coal.

4. **Requisition for a Deed.**—Adam Bede and his wife, Mary, live in Madison, Wisconsin, on the southeast corner of State street and Murray street. The lot is 100 feet square. They occupy the house situated thereon as their home. They have mortgaged the place to secure a note for $5,000, given by Bede to the Bank of Wisconsin, due in 2 years with interest at 7 per cent. This mortgage is recorded in Book 50 of Mortgages at page 100.

Noah Brown has contracted to purchase the place for $20,000 and as part payment is to assume the payment of the mortgage debt. Bede has other lands nearby, and has stipulated that the purchaser shall take a deed containing a condition against using the land for anything except residence purposes.

Prepare a deed of conveyance to comply with the contract and let it contain six covenants for title, expressed not implied. The deed is to be in such form as to terminate whatever rights Mary Bede may have in the land, but she is not to be bound by the covenants.   Have   the   deed   properly   executed   and acknowledged.

FORM OF DEED (1)

Form of deed for conveyance of an estate in fee simple to commence at the death of the grantor. J. L. Thorndike, 3 Massachusetts Law Quarterly 121 (Feb. 1918). (a)

KNOW ALL MEN that I, Samuel Hawes, of, etc., in consideration of the sum of $650 (six hundred and fifty dollars) to me paid by Elizabeth Cook of, etc. (hereinafter called the Grantee), the receipt whereof is hereby acknowledged, do hereby grant unto the Grantee and her heirs and assigns all those two pieces of land situate, etc., first a piece of land, etc., secondly, etc.

TO HAVE AND TO HOLD the premises hereby granted unto the Grantee and her heirs and assigns to my use during my life without impeachment of waste (b), (but so that I shall not be at liberty to cut the wood on the last-mentioned piece of land) (c).   And after my death (upon condition that she continues to keep my house and take care of me during her and my joint lives) to her and their use forever.

And I do hereby covenant with the Grantee that I am lawfully seized of the premises hereby granted. That they are free from all incumbrances. That I have good right to grant the same as aforesaid, and that I will warrant and defend the same against the lawful claims and demands of all persons.

(a) This form, including the clauses in brackets, carries into effect the intention of the deed in Trafton v. Hawes, 102 Mass. 228, 231; without involving the questions raised in that case. Cf. also the conveyances in Gale v. Coburn, 18 Pick. 397, and Brewer v. Hardy, 22 Pick. 376.

(b) As to impeachment of waste, see Wms. Settlement, 185, 228, 231; Wms. R. P. (13th ed.) 23-25; (22nd ed.) 116-118; 1 Tiffany, R. P. ss. 246, 252; Noyes v. Stone, 163 Mass. 490; Young v. Haviland, 215 Mass. 120, 124; Billings v. Taylor, 10 Pick. 460.

(c) For other forms of restriction as to waste, see 2 Key & Elph. Conv. (3rd ed.) 576; (9th ed.) 656.

For deed reserving a life estate to grantor—Buck v. Garber, 261 Ill. 378.

IN WITNESS WHEREOF I, the said Samuel Hawes, have hereunto set my hand and seal the .... day of ...., in the year ....
Signed, sealed and delivered   Samuel Hawes (Seal)
in the presence of
    A. B.

FORM OF DEED (2)

Form of deed for conveyance of an estate for life with remainder in fee simple, deriving its effect from the Statute of Uses. J. L. Thorndike, 3 Massachusetts Law Quarterly 122 (Feb., 1918). (a)

KNOW ALL MEN that I, E. F., of, etc., in consideration of $1,000 (one thousand dollars) to me paid by A. R., of, etc. (hereinafter called the Grantee), the receipt whereof is hereby acknowledged, do hereby grant unto the Grantee and his heirs all that piece of land situate, etc. (Description.)

TO HAVE AND TO HOLD the premises hereby granted unto the Grantee and his heirs to the use of the Grantee during his life without impeachment of waste. And after his death to the use of his two sons, D. R., of, etc., and G. R., of etc., and their heirs and assigns. In case either of said sons shall die without issue in the lifetime of their father, then all of the said lands shall go to the survivor.

And I do hereby covenant (b) with the Grantee (c) that the premises hereby granted are free from all incumbrances

---

(a) Cf. Chenery v. Stevens, 97 Mass. 77, 85; Burton's Compendium, 47.

(b) The liability of the heirs of the covenantor is regulated wholly by statute, and it is not necessary to mention them (Hall v. Bumstead, 20 Pick. 2, 3; Bullard v. Moor, 158 Mass. 418, 425).

(c) The covenants should be made with the grantee to uses and then they enure with the land to the successive cestuis que use (5 Byth. & J. Conv. (4th ed.) 278; 1 Dav. Conv. (4th ed.) 116. It is not necessary to mention the heirs or assigns of this grantee.

A stranger to those mentioned in the premises of deed may be introduced in the habendum as a grantee in remainder. I Wood on Conveyancing (6 Eng. ed., Hab., p. 336); McCullock v. Holmes (1892), 111 Mo. 445, 19 S. W. 1096.

made or suffered by me, and that I will warrant and defend the same against the lawful claims and demands of all persons claiming through or under me.

IN WITNESS WHEREOF, etc.

E. F.   (Seal)

Ordinary Form of Corporate Deed   (3)

THIS INDENTURE, Made this 9th day of October, 1920, between The Portage Park Land Company, a corporation of Michigan, and Augustine W. Farr and Jessie E. Farr, his wife, both of the County of Manistee and State of Michigan, parties of the first part, and Isabel Bevier and Martha J. Kyle, of the County of Champaign, State of Illinois, parties of the second part,

WITNESSETH, That the said parties of the first part for and in consideration of the sum of $10.00 and other valuable considerations to them in hand paid by the said parties of the second part, the receipt whereof is hereby confessed and acknowledged, do by these presents, grant, bargain, sell, remise, release and forever warrant unto the parties of the second part and to their heirs and assigns forever, all that certain piece or parcel of land situated in the County of Manistee and State of Michigan and known and described as follows:

Lot 3, Block 1 of Portage Park Resort, according to the recorded plat thereof, and located in Township 23, Range 16 West, in Manistee County, Michigan,

together with all and singular hereditaments and appurtenances thereunto belonging or in any wise pertaining, to have and to hold the said premises to the parties of the second part and to their heirs and assigns, to the sole and proper use of the said parties of the second part, their heirs and assigns forever.

IN WITNESS WHEREOF the said parties of the first part have caused this instrument to be executed,

Rec & Ref Lands Company Cor

the Portage Park Land Company under the hands of
its Vice-President and Secretary and under its corporate seal, and the said Augustine W. Farr and
Jessie E. Farr under their respective hands and seals
this 9th day of October, A. D. 1920.

THE PORTAGE PARK LAND COMPANY,

By Elwyn W. Seymour, Vice-President.

Attest:　　　　　　　　　Jessie E. Farr　　　　(Seal)
　　R. F. Church,　　　　　Augustine W. Farr　(Seal)
　　　Secretary.

Signed, sealed and delivered
by Elwyn W. Seymour,
in the presence of
　　Geo. I. Hicks,
　　Mina Hagberg.

Signed, sealed and delivered　Signed, sealed and delivered
by R. F. Church,　　　　　　by Augustine W. Farr and Jessie
in the presence of　　·　　　E. Farr in the presence of
　　Geo. I. Hicks,　　　　　　　George W. Farr,
　　Mina Hagberg.　　　　　　　Jessie Farr.

State of Illinois ⎱
County of Cook ⎰ ss.

On this 9th day of October, A. D. 1920, before me
appeared Elwyn W. Seymour and R. F. Church respectively, to me personally known, who being by me
duly sworn, depose that Elwyn W. Seymour is Vice-
President of The Portage Park Land Company and
R. F. Church is Secretary of said company, the corporation which executed the foregoing instrument, and
that the seal affixed to said instrument is the corporate seal of said corporation, and that said instrument
was signed and sealed in behalf of said corporation by
authority of its Board of Directors.

IN WITNESS WHEREOF, I have hereunto set my

hand and notarial seal this 9th day of October, A. D. 1920.

George I. Hicks,
Notary Public.

My commission expires April 2, 1923.

(Seal)

State of Illinois ⎰ ss.
County of Cook ⎱

I, George I. Hicks, a Notary Public in and for said County and State, do hereby certify that Elwyn W. Seymour and R. F. Church known to me to be respectively the same persons whose names are subscribed to the foregoing instrument, and personally known to me to be the Vice-President and Secretary respectively of the Portage Park Land Company, appeared before me this day in person and acknowledged that they signed, sealed and delivered said instrument as their free and voluntary act as such officers respectively and as the free and voluntary act of said company for the uses and purposes therein set forth.

Given under my hand and notarial seal this 9th day of October, A. D. 1920.

George I. Hicks,
Notary Public.

(Seal)

My commission expires April 2, 1923.

States of Michigan ⎰ ss.
County of Manistee ⎱

On this 20th day of December, A. D. 1920, personally appeared before me Augustine W. Farr and Jessie E. Farr, his wife, to me known to be the persons described in and who executed the foregoing instrument and acknowledged that they signed, sealed and delivered the said instrument as their free and voluntary act for the uses and purposes therein set forth.

Given under my hand and notarial seal this 20th day of December, A. D. 1920.

Laura H. Johnson,
Notary Public.

My commission expires June 22, 1924.
(Seal)

CHAPTER VI

REAL ESTATE MORTGAGES AND TRUST DEEDS

Value of the Security.—One about to lend money on the security of a real estate mortgage should satisfy himself in the first place as to the market value of the property, and also as to the status of the tenants and occupiers; whether the tenant, if any, pays his rent regularly and whether he has paid it far in advance. While there is no hard and fast rule as to what is sufficient security, business prudence would ordinarily suggest that on vacant unimproved property money loaned should not exceed one-third of the market value; on residence property one-half and on well situated business property three-fourths of the value.

The lender should make almost as careful an examination of the title as a purchaser, although in some details it need not be quite so particular. The entire expense of such examination is always put upon the borrower.

If one is asked to loan money on property at a distance, he should consider what he will have to do in event that foreclosure is necessary. He should contemplate the possibility that he may have to employ an attorney in a distant state on the recommendation of others; that he may have to take in the property for the debt with no reliable information as to its value. He should also consider the difficulty of finding reliable tenants and enforcing his rights against them if he has to take over property in a distant place.

Form and Essentials of Mortgage.—A mortgage is in form simply a conveyance on condition subsequent. If a deed describes the parties, the debt or obligation secured, and the property conveyed, it is sufficient as a valid mortgage. In some states the statutes provide a short and simple form, but longer forms are usually employed.

The numerous and stringent provisions for repairing, insuring and preserving the security are not to be looked upon as oppressive or adverse to the mortgagor. They are intended merely to render the security safer, more enforcible and marketable. The mortagee is not allowed to enforce any forfeiture or get anything beyond his principal, interest and expenses. No clog or fetter on the mortgagor's right to redeem is valid.

The characteristic feature of a mortgage deed is the condition subsequent or proviso for defeasance of the transfer by payment of the debt or performance of the obligation secured. Sometimes a separate instrument of defeasance is employed, but this seems undesirable. The form of condition subsequent or proviso of a mortgage deed is somewhat as follows:

"John Doe conveys to Richard Roe and his heirs the following described property; provided always, that if the mortgagor shall pay to the mortgagee $5,000 upon the first day of January, 1921, then the whole title and estate hereby granted shall cease and determine, and the mortgagor shall be revested with his former title and estate."

It is sometimes provided that if the notes are paid the mortgage shall become null and void, but what is meant is that the lien or security interest of the lender or creditor shall cease.

If a conveyance of property is made as security for debt, whatever its form, equity will hold it to be a mortgage. A clause of defeasance or proviso for redemption is not necessary. Even if a deed be absolute on its face, the intent to have it stand as security may be shown by parol evidence. In some states a deed of trust running to a third person as trustee, with power to sell in default of payment, is employed in place of a mortgage purporting to convey the security directly to the creditor. In mortgages to secure bondholders or numerous creditors, the trust deed is usually employed. A trust deed to secure a debt is in legal effect a mortgage, although in some states it may be more easily foreclosed.

The formalities of execution of a mortgage are the same as those of deeds. Many of the provisions are the same as those of land contracts where credit is given, as the relation of vendor and purchaser is very similar to that of mortgagee and mortgagor.

Parties.—It is convenient oftentimes to describe the mortagor as "the borrower," the mortgagee as "the lender." To avoid repetition these terms may be stated to include their executors, administrators and assigns. The wife of the mortgagor should join to bar her dower and waive or release her homestead rights. In Illinois this waiver of homestead must be contained both in the deed and in the certificate of acknowledgment.

Recitals.—In the case of corporate mortgages and deeds of trust, it is customary to recite resolutions of the stockholders and directors, showing that the mortgage and the indebtedness secured are duly authorized. In the case of a second mortgage, it may be well to recite the existing encumbrance and the amount due or secured.

Covenant for Payment.—A mortgage usually contains a covenant for payment of the principal debt with interest at a specified rate. A copy of the note or obligation secured is often set forth, although this is not necessary as long as the indebtedness is identified. The mortgage may provide that it shall stand as security for all renewals and extensions of the original indebtedness and for all subsequent advances and other liabilities of the mortgagor, due or to become due, or which may be thereafter contracted, and that no change in the evidence of the indebtedness shall affect the security. It is to the advantage of the mortgagor, however, to have the amount of the indebtedness definitely fixed, so that he may be able to deal with his equity of redemption.

Power of Sale.—In some jurisdictions foreclosure may be effected under a power of sale by a public auction or sale upon due notice as prescribed by the mortgage or by statute, without suit in court. In other states foreclosure under a power of sale contained in the mortgage is not allowed, but the mortgagee must apply to a court to fix a limited time for the mortgagor to pay off the debt and to redeem the property before it is sold at a judicial sale. Even if the power of sale is invalid, it will not affect the validity of the mortgage. In any case it is difficult to produce to a future purchaser satisfactory evidence that the conditions and events giving rise to the power of sale have happened and that junior liens are barred, so that foreclosure by suit is ordinarily preferable.

Covenant to Insure.—The mortgagor will ordinarily covenant to keep the buildings and improvements insured against loss by fire and possibly by tornado, for the benefit of the holder of the note and mortgage, the loss, if any under the policy, to be payable to such holder as his interest may appear. It may also be provided that insurance as to the interest of the mortgagee shall not be invalidated by any act or neglect of the mortgagor, or the owner of the property described, nor by any change in his title. It may also be provided that the insurance policy shall be delivered to the mortgagee and also receipts for premiums from time to time. The mortgagee may be authorized to insure in case of the mortgagor's failure to do so, and add the same to the indebtedness secured.

Taxes.—The mortgagor covenants to pay all taxes, assessments and liens which may attach to the premises, and the mortgagee or trustee will be authorized to pay these without previous notice, and such payments shall become additional indebtedness under the mortgage.

Acceleration Clause.—It is usual to provide that in the event of the failure on the part of the mortgagor to perform his agreements, or to pay any part of the principal or interest when due, or in case of waste or non-payment of taxes and assessments, or neglect to insure and keep insured the buildings on the mortgaged premises, that the whole amount of principal and accrued interest shall become immediately due and payable at the option of the holder, and the mortgage may be foreclosed.

Other provisions such as those relating to possession by the mortgagor until default, repairs, power in the borrower to sell portions of the mortgaged premises and apply the proceeds in part payment, will be indicated in the following summary or outline of a mortgage:

OUTLINE OF MORTGAGE DEED

1. Names and description of parties and recitals (if any).

2. A. B., the borrower, grants and conveys by way of mortgage, or mortgages to C. D., the lender, or

mortgagee and his heirs as security for a certain debt or note (described below), the following described property: (Insert description).

3. Condition subsequent or proviso for defeasance upon payment at a certain date and performance of subsidiary covenants.

4. Covenant for payment of principal debt with interest at .... per cent (reducible to .... per cent on prompt payment). (Set out copy of note or description of indebtedness secured.)

5. Insurance of improvements by mortgagor for benefit of mortgagee and mortgagor for two-thirds of the cash value, loss payable to the mortgagee. Power to the mortgagee to insure and add the expense to the principal. In case of loss, proceeds of insurance to be credited on debt or expended in repair at option of holder of mortgage.

6. Taxes and assessments levied against the property or against the mortgage debt to be paid by the mortgagor.

7. Defense of suits relating to the property to be made by the mortgagor.

8. Capitalization or compounding of interest in arrears. If interest is in arrears for fourteen days it shall be added to the principal's moneys hereby secured and shall bear interest like the principal. This may not be valid in many states.

9. Acceleratation clause: the mortgagee to have the right to call the whole amount on default of payment of any interest or principal installment or any breach of any of the mortgagor's covenants.

10. Provision for attorneys' fees and other expenses on foreclosure.

11. Power of sale, at public or private sale on default and notice to mortgagor. (In some states a mort-

gage must be foreclosed by suit in court and a power
of sale is invalid.)

12. Covenant by mortgagor to keep buildings in
good repair and maintain the property.

13. Privilege of partial payments before maturity of
mortgage, not less than ...... dollars at any one time
payable at times when interest is due.

14. If the borrower at any time sells a part of the
premises hereby conveyed at a price approved by the
mortgagee (or at ...... dollars per acre), then the
mortgagee, provided that all interest due shall have
been paid down to preceding half yearly date), will
join in the conveyance to the purchaser, and accept the
proceeds toward discharge of the mortgage.

16. The wife of the mortgagor should join with him
to bar her dower and release and waive homestead
rights. In Illinois the waiver must appear in the body
of the deed and also in the acknowledgment.

17. Covenants for title.

18. Execution and acknowledgment by the mortgagors.

Assignment of Mortgage.—An assignment of mortgage involves first the assignment of the debt secured
by the mortgage, and second, the conveyance or transfer of the security interest in the mortgaged property
subject to the right of redemption. It is well, if possible, to have the mortgagor join in the assignment,
or at least to give notice to him of the assignment, as
payments made by him to the original mortgagee without notice of the assignment are valid. An assignment
of the mortgage alone will not transfer the note, but an
assignment of the debt carries the security with it in
equity. (Tobin v. Tobin, 139 Wisconsin, 494, 499.) The
assignment should be recorded.

If a mortgagee is unwilling to continue or renew

the mortgage and calls in his money, the mortgagor may be able to procure another lender to advance the money and take an assignment or transfer of the existing mortgage security and debt. The assignee will thereby get the same priority as the first mortgagee, even though the mortgagor may have encumbered the equity of redemption and could not now give a first mortgage.

Form of Assignment of Mortgage

For value received, I, A. B., of Champaign, Illinois, hereby assign to C. D., of the same place, that certain mortgage executed to me by E. F., and wife, the ...... day of ...., 19...., and recorded in volume .... of Mortgages at page ......; together with the note and obligation or indebtedness thereby secured in the amount of $..........

Witness my hand and seal this ...... day of ...... 1920.

(Signed)   A. B.   (Seal)

In the presence of

....

....

(Certificate of Acknowledgment)

Release of Equity of Redemption.—One sort of "foreclosure" that is sometimes attempted is by the mortgagee taking release and conveyance from the mortgagor of his equity of redemption in satisfaction of the debt. This is a dangerous way to avoid the expense of foreclosure suit, even if the mortgagor is willing to do it. In order to support a transfer from the mortgagor to the mortgagee, cutting off the equity of redemption, it must be shown that no advantage was taken of the debtor to drive a hard bargain. (Young v. Miner, 141

Wisconsin, 501, 508; Coates v. Marsden, 142 Wisconsin, 106, 110.) Public policy does not permit the borrower to agree in advance to any forfeiture of his rights of redemption, but after default the extinguishment is permitted if fairly made. There is, moreover, great danger to the mortgagee that he will lose his priority and let in judgment liens and second mortgages by merging his mortgage in the equity of redemption.

Satisfaction of Mortgage.—In "title" states, a release, discharge or satisfaction of mortgage is usually made by a deed of quit-claim or release of the mortgaged premises, referring to the volume and page of the mortgage records. In "lien" states, a release is often made in the form of a certificate or acknowledgment that the debt has been paid and the mortgage discharged, executed under seal and acknowledged. In many states a mortgage may be released by an entry on the margin of the record (Tiffany, Legal and Business Forms, p. 990).

REQUISITION FOR MORTGAGE

The Adam Bede Company is an Illinois corporation doing business here. John Doe is the president, James Roe the secretary, and Joseph Roe the treasurer of the company.

The corporation wishes to borrow $20,000 from John Hardy. It is agreed that the company shall give its note, payable four years after date, with interest payable semi-annually at the rate of six per cent (6%) per annum, the note to be secured by a mortgage trust deed upon a parcel of the company's realty. It is agreed that the company shall have the privilege of making payments upon the principal at any time when, according to the terms of the loan, interest becomes due and payable, such payments to be in amounts of

One Thousand Dollars ($1,000) or any multiple thereof; that the company shall remain in possession of the premises, and shall keep them insured for Hardy's benefit and pay the taxes; if interest, taxes or insurance premiums are not paid promptly, your client (Mr. Hardy) wishes to be able either to pay same and have such amounts become additional charges upon the realty, or to be in a position to take steps under the mortgage to collect the whole amount loaned at once, although the four years may not have elapsed. He wishes also that a power of sale may be provided for, and attorney's fee on foreclosure. The company agrees to these terms, so far as they are valid by the law of the state.

Draw the note and mortgage or trust deed in accordance with the foregoing facts.

> Acceleration Clause, Hoodless v. Reid, 112 Ill. 105;
> Power of Sale, Ill. Statutes, Chap. 95, Sec. 22;
> Attorney's Fee, Abbott v. Stone, 172 Ill. 634; Unity
> Co. v. Equitable Tr. Co., 204 Ill. 595.

FORM OF MORTGAGE

THIS INDENTURE, made this first day of March, One Thousand Nine Hundred and Eighteen, between the Adam Bede Company, an Illinois Corporation, having its principal place of business at Chicago, Illinois, the mortgagor or borrower (also the wife of borrower, if an individual), and John Hardy, mortgagee or lender.

WITNESSETH, That the borrower for and in consideration of the sum of Twenty Thousand ($20,000) Dollars, now lent by the mortgagee to the borrower, the receipt of which sum the borrower hereby acknowledges, the borrower hereby grants, bargains, sells, conveys and warrants to the mortgagee and his heirs forever, by way of mortgage,

All that tract and parcel of land lying and being in the County of Cook and State of Illinois, described as follows, to wit: (Insert description)

Hereby releasing and waiving all rights under and by virtue of the Homestead Exemption Laws of this State (in case of an individual);

To have and to hold the same, together with all appurtenances, unto the said party of the second part, his heirs and assigns forever, to secure the herein mentioned note and covenants.

It is hereby provided that if the said borrower shall well and truly pay the said sum of Twenty Thousand ($20,000) Dollars, according to the note of even date herewith, on the first day of March, 1922, with interest thereon from the date hereof at the rate of six per cent (6%) per annum, the first payment of interest to be made on the first day of June ensuing the date hereof, and thereafter quarterly on the first days of September, December, June and March, according to the terms and conditions of that certain note executed by said borrower to said mortgagee, bearing even date herewith, and shall well and truly keep and perform all the covenants and agreements herein contained, then this deed is to be null and void, and the premises hereby conveyed and mortgaged shall, at the request and cost of the borrower, be duly reconveyed to him, his heirs or assigns or released from this mortgage.

The said borrower does covenant and agree to pay the sums of money above specified and the interest thereon at the times and in the manner above mentioned;

To pay all taxes and assessments of every nature that may be assessed on the said premises or any part thereof, previous to the day appointed for the sale of land for such taxes;

And to repair and keep in repair, and to insure and keep insured, all buildings on the premises herein conveyed against loss or damage by fire or lightning, for at least the sum of Five Thousand ($5,000) Dollars, in the joint names of the borrower and mortgagee, loss payable to said mortgagee to the amount then unpaid on and secured by this mortgage. The borrower will forthwith deliver to the mortgagee the policy or policies of insurance and receipts for premiums. All money received on any insurance policy shall be applied to the restoration of the premises or at the option of the mortgagee can be applied towards the discharge of the mortgage debt.

In case of failure to pay said taxes or to keep said buildings so insured or repaired, the mortgagee may at his option pay and discharge such taxes and effect such insurance on said buildings, or make needed repairs, and the sums which may be so paid by the mortgagee shall draw interest from the time of such payment at the rate of seven per cent (7%) per annum and shall be secured in the same manner as the original debt by this mortgage.

The borrower shall have the privilege of paying off the principal money at any time when the interest is due and payable, in amounts of not less than Five Hundred ($500) Dollars, or any multiple thereof.

If default shall be made in any of the conditions or covenants herein, or in said note contained, and such default shall continue for the space of thirty days the whole of said principal sum and all accrued interest thereon shall thereupon become due and payable without notice to said borrower, his heirs or assigns.

The said borrower, in case of such default and the continuance thereof as aforesaid, does hereby authorize and empower the mortgagee and his assigns, to sell said premises at public auction and convey the same to the purchaser, and of the moneys arising from such sale to retain the principal and interest then due on said note, together with all expenses for taxes or insurance, with the interest thereon, and all costs and charges and ten per cent (10%) as attorneys' fees, and pay the surplus, if any, to the borrower.

The provisions hereof shall extend to and be binding upon the respective parties, their heirs, executors, administrators or assigns.

And the said borrower does hereby agree to pay to the said mortgagee, in case of foreclosure of this mortgage by action, a reasonable sum as attorney's fee, which shall be included in the judgment and paid out of the proceeds of sale thereunder.

IN WITNESS WHEREOF the said Adam Bede Company has hereunto caused its corporate name to be signed and its corporate seal to be affixed by its officers thereunto duly authorized.

ADAM BEDE COMPANY, by

John Doe, President

James Roe, Secretary

(Corporate seal.)

Signed, sealed and delivered

in the presence of

James Doe   Richard Roe.

FORM OF MORTGAGE TO SECURE PROMISSORY NOTES
Clarke v. *Hunter,* 83 Ill. App. p. 100

Provisions Included.—By reference to the following mortgage it will be seen that its provisions are that it is made to secure the payment of one principal note of $5,000, payable on the first of March, 1894, and ten interest notes for $150.00 each, payable in succession every six months, to the order of Edward T. Oliver;

that if the notes are paid when due the mortgage shall be void, otherwise to remain in force, provided that the neglect or refusal to pay any of the notes when due, or in case of waste or non-payment of taxes and assessments, or the neglect to insure and keep insured the building on the mortgaged premises, in the amount of at least nine hundred dollars, in such company as the legal holder of the note may desire, for the benefit of the holder, it is agreed will render the principal note with accrued interest immediately due and payable at the option of the legal holder, and that the mortgage may be foreclosed. Then provisions follow for filing a bill to foreclose the mortgage for the amount due upon the notes and for costs, taxes, assessments, insurance, attorney's fees, and money expended under other provisions of the mortgage, including a reasonable solicitor's fee, not exceeding five per cent, to be taxed as other costs.

Conveyance by Way of Mortgage.
The mortgagors, John B. Hunter and Elizabeth E. Hunter, his wife, of the county of Sangamon and State of Illinois, for and in consideration of five thousand dollars in hand paid, mortgage and warrant to Edward T. Oliver, of the county of Sangamon, the following described real estate, to wit:

Description.
The southwest quarter of section eleven (11), east half of the northwest quarter of section fourteen (14), and eighteen (18) acres of the east half of southwest quarter, section twelve (12), and all in township seventeen, north of range two, west of third principal meridian, 258 acres in all, together with all the rents, issues and profits thereof, situated in the county of Logan, in the State of Illinois,

Waiver of Homestead.
hereby releasing and waiving all rights under and by virtue of the Homestead Exemption laws of this State,

Notes and obligations secured.

to secure the payment of eleven promissory notes of even date herewith, executed by said John B. Hunter and payable to the order of said Edward T. Oliver, as follows: One principal note for the sum of five thousand dollars, payable on the first day of March, 1894; one interest note for the sum of one hundred and fifty dollars, payable on the first day of September, 1889; and nine interest notes for the sum of one hundred and fifty dollars each, and payable, respectively on March 1, 1890; September 1, 1890; March 1, 1891; September 1, 1891; March 1, 1892; September 1, 1892; March 1, 1893; September, 1893; all bearing interest at the rate of eight per cent per annum from maturity until paid, payable semi-annually.

Condition Subsequent.

Now if said notes are paid when due according to their tenor and effect, then this mortgage to be null and void, otherwise to be and remain in full force;

Acceleration Clause.

provided that the neglect or refusal to pay any of said notes when due or in case of waste or non-payment of taxes and assessments, or the neglect to insure and to keep insured the buildings on said premises in the amount of at least ($900) nine hundred dollars, in such company as the legal holder of said note may direct, for the benefit of such legal holder does, it is hereby agreed, render the principal note with all accrued interest thereon immediately due and payable by the said John B. Hunter, at the option of the legal holder of said note, and this mortgage may be foreclosed.

Power of Attorney to Confess Judgment for Indebtedness and of Foreclosure.

And the said John B. Hunter and Elizabeth Hunter hereby waive notice of such option and authorize and empower Geo. M. Brinkerhoff, or any attorney of any court of record, to enter the appearance of the said John B. Hunter and Elizabeth E. Hunter, upon the filing of any bill to foreclose this mortgage in any court having jurisdiction thereof, and to file an answer for the said John B. Hunter and Elizabeth E. Hunter, stating the amount that may then be due and owing on said notes in this mortgage mentioned, for principal and interest, also for costs, taxes, assessments, insurance, attorney's fees and other money expended under the provisions contained herein, whether the same be due by the terms of this mortgage or by the option of the said Edward T. Oliver, his heirs, executors, administrators or assigns, and to consent and agree to a decree being entered for the amount therein stated to be so due and owing, in favor of the said Edward T. Oliver, his heirs, executors, administrators or assigns; that no appeal shall be taken from such decree, and no writ of error.

Appointment of Receiver.

In the case of the filing of any bill to foreclose this mortgage, this court may appoint Geo. M. Brinkerhoff, or any competent person, receiver with power to collect the rents and profits arising out of said premises during the pendency of such foreclosure suit and until the right to redeem said premises expires and such rents and profits so collected shall be applied to the payment of taxes, insurance, or toward the payment of such indebtedness upon the foreclosure of this mortgage by proceedings in court; and in case said premises are occupied by the mortgagors, they hereby agree to become tenants of such receiver or to surrender immediate possession of said premises to him.

Attorney's fees.

The cost of such foreclosure shall be paid by the mortgagors, which shall include a reasonable solicitors' fee, not to exceed five per cent, to be taxed by the court and collected as other costs.

Dated this twentieth day of February, A. D. 1889.

IN WITNESS WHEREOF, the parties
hereto have set their hands and seals this
20th day of February, A. D. 1889.

            John Hunter   (Seal)
  (Seal)   Elizabeth Hunter   (Seal)

Signed, sealed and delivered in the presence
of Lewis Grubb.

(Acknowledgment.)

CHAPTER VII

CHATTEL MORTGAGES AND CONDITIONAL SALES

Methods.—Dealers in personal property who sell on the installment plan usually adopt one of four ways of protecting themselves in case of default, namely: (1) A provision that title is to remain in the seller until the buyer has performed his part of the agreement; (2) a lease with right to acquire title upon full payment of the purchase price; (3) the sale to the purchaser and an immediate resale by way of chattel mortgage to the seller; (4) conveyance to a trustee in trust to hold the title pending performance of the contract and subject to its provisions. The purpose is the same in all of these transactions. In a number of states it is held that the form first mentioned shall not be enforced according to its terms but will be regarded as a sale with a chattel mortgage back to secure the unpaid purchase price, and the same formalities have to be observed.

A contract for the sale of a piano or sewing machine by means of monthly installments of rents is held to be a conditional sale, notwithstanding the agreement may be called a lease. (Singer Mfg. Co. v. Ellington, 103 Ill. App. 517.) In some states it is possible to draw a conditional sale so that it shall not amount to a chattel mortgage. (5 Ruling Case Law Chattel Mortgages, pp. 385, 386; 154 Wis. 490. Tiffany Legal Forms, pp. 699, 1200. Haring Conditional Sales, p. 339.)

Chattel Mortgages Compared to a Pledge.—A chattel mortgage often furnishes a convenient basis of credit to men of small capital who cannot furnish other security. Like a real estate mortgage it usually takes the form of a transfer of title to the lender subject to a condition· subsequent that the transfer may be defeated by payment at a certain date. The chattel mortgage is then in form a bill of sale on condition subsequent.

The advantage of a chattel mortgage over a pledge of the goods• lies in the fact that the mortgagor is enabled to keep possession, use and benefit of the goods. In the case of a mortgage upon a stock in trade, he may even be allowed to market and sell the goods in the course of business and replace them with other property of like kind from the proceeds of that sold. The security of the mortgagee is not dependent upon possession like the lien of a pledgee, where the goods must be deposited with the creditor.

Recording Acts.—Since the very object of mortgage is to do away with the necessity of change of possession, filing and recording acts have been passed, by which public notice of chattel mortgages is given, and these records may be scanned by business men in giving credit to purchasers. These public records give constructive notice to all dealing with the property, and are a substitute for delivery and continuous change of possession, which is essential to make a transfer by sale operative against subsequent creditors and purchasers. A chattel mortgage, duly recorded, even has priority over liens for storage or repairs. Statutes are common making it criminal in the mortgagor fraudulently to sell, remove, or dispose of mortgaged personal property.

Formalities of Execution.—While a mortgage is valid between the parties without filing or recording, the statutory formalities of execution must be strictly observed to give priority of lien against creditors and third parties. These formalities are usually an acknowledgment of the bill of sale before some justice of the peace or notary public, stating the amount of the debt or obligation, with an affidavit of good faith to the effect that the transfer is not made to hinder, delay or defraud creditors, and the filing of the mortgage at the office of the city clerk or the county recorder's office in the county where the debtor resides, or where the mortgaged property is situated, or both. Removal of the property may necessitate a new filing and recordation. Actual possession by the mortgagee cures defects in execution and renders filing or recording immaterial.

Renewal.—The continuance of the lien of a chattel mortgage is often limited by statute to one or two years, and it may be necessary that the mortgage be renewed or refiled every year. The chattel mortgage under some statutes is renewed by the filing of an affidavit made by the mortgagee setting forth the names of the mortgagor and mortgagee, the date of filing the mortgage and the amount of debt owing at the date of making the affidavit, together with an affidavit that the mortgage was neither made or renewed to hinder or defraud creditors or subsequent mortgagees. The statutes of each state must be consulted as to the making and renewal of chattel mortgages.

A note secured by chattel mortgage should contain a statement that "this note is secured by chattel mortgage."

Summary of Usual Provisions of Chattel Mortgage

1. Bill of Sale. A. B. assigns to C. D. all the chattels described in the schedule annexed, by way of security for the payment of the sum of $...............

evidenced by a note of ....date, a copy of which follows:

2. Covenant to pay the indebtedness.

3. Proviso or defeasance clause.

4. Provision that the mortgagor may retain possession until default or until the mortgagee feels himself insecure.

5. Provision for taking of possession by mortgagee in case of default or in case of feeling himself insecure. Power to enter with or without force or process of court and remove the goods.

6. That the mortgagor will keep the goods insured; that he will keep them in good repair and condition and will replace any that may be worn out.

7. Power of sale, either by public auction or private sale, on or off the premises, with liberty in the mortgagee to buy in at any sale by auction.

8. That the mortgagor will not remove said chattels except to repair them, and that mortgagee may enter to view their condition.

9. Mortgagor to pay attorney's fees and all expenses in case of default.

10. Execution, acknowledgment and affidavits.

Future or After Acquired Property; Stock in Trade. —Retention of possession often involves consumption or sale of goods with the right to replace them. This gives rise to great difficulties and conflict of authority as to whether the mortgage will cover such "future goods." Take the case of a mortgage of the floating stock in trade and of such merchandise as one may thereafter acquire and use in connection with his particular line of business, reserving the power to sell in the regular course of trade, and to make additions to the stock, which shall become at once subject to the mortgage. In some states the reservation of a power of sale by the mortgagor to sell in the usual course of business invalidates the lien against creditors and in others requires special provisions. A man cannot grant title by sale or mortgage to property of which he has not yet acquired title. At law some new act is required in ratification or furtherance of the mortgage to specify the property and appropriate it to the mortgage, as by reducing the property to possession or recording a new mortgage when the after acquired chattels have come into existence. The mortgagee must take possession before the claims of third persons attach, otherwise the mortgage creates no lien. In equity, however, it has been held that an equitable lien attaches immediately upon the property coming into existence and adheres to it for the security of the mortgagee, as against the mortgagor and all persons claiming through him with notice, voluntarily or in bankruptcy. The prior record in some states gives notice what property is subject to the lien, and the lien of the mortgage will prevail over creditors, even though the mortgagor or mortgagee do no further act to perfect the lien after the property has been acquired. (I Cobbey, Chattel Mortgages, pp. 389, 515.)

Foreclosure by Extrajudicial Sale.—Mortgage being a "higher" security than pledge, it would seem that the mortgagee ought to be able to foreclose the mortgagor's right of redemption when the debt becomes due, by a sale of the property made in the manner and upon the notice requisite in pledge, without invoking the authority of a court. Owing to the conflicting views of mortgage at law and in equity this is not universally admitted, and the right of the mortgagee in respect to enforcement may be inferior to that of the pledgee. The rule is invariable as to mortgages of real property that the mortgagee must obtain a judicial decree of sale to foreclose the equitable right of redemption, unless the mortgage deed provides an express power of sale. In the case of personal property mortgages, where the value may not justify expensive litigation, the mortgagee ought to have an implied power conferred upon him by law and equity to make a sale to satisfy the debt equally with a pledgee.

Even where an express power of sale is conferred by the mortgage instrument, the sale must be at public auction after reasonable notice, and the mortgagee cannot himself become a purchaser at his own sale though fairly conducted, unless he is expressly authorized to do so. There is no redemption from sale under power unless it be given by statute. Foreclosure by sale on judicial sentence may be advisable in any case, if there be a dispute as to the amount of debt, or the rights of junior lienors and sub-vendees be involved. The surplus, if the proceeds of the sale exceed the debt, must be accounted for to the mortgagor; thus forfeiture is avoided and the mortgagee recovers only his just due. Sale before foreclosure is conversion, though recovery would be limited to the value, less the amount of the mortgage debt, as in case of conversion by a pledgee.

Conditional Sale Problem.—How could you draw a conditional sale contract in your state so as to protect the seller, and so that it shall not be a chattel mortgage? Insert provisions that (1) title shall remain in the seller until the full amount of the purchase price is paid; (2) that the seller may retake the goods after buyer fails to pay any installment or becomes insolvent; (3) that the property shall be at the sole risk of the buyer and insured by him; (4) no removal or alienation; (5) seller may keep payments for use in case of retaking; (6) add necessary signatures, acknowledgments, or other formalities.

Requisition for Chattel Mortgage.—John Bede and James Bede, partners under the firm name of Bede Brothers, wish to borrow $10,000 for three years, giving as security a mortgage on the stock of goods used by them in their retail hardware business at 100 State Street, Urbana, Illinois. Your client, Richard Roe, is willing to lend the money, but wishes the mortgage drawn so that it will not be subject to successful attack by other creditors of Bede Bros. It is agreed that, *if it can be done without endangering the security,* the mortgagors are to continue their business, buying and selling goods as before the giving of the mortgage, and new goods added to the stock are to be covered by the mortgage.

Your client, Richard Roe, wishes you to draw a note and mortgage which *will fully protect his security in any event,* but which will express and carry out the above agreement as to possession, etc., as far as it may be done under the law of your state without endangering the security of the mortgage.

You are employed to prepare such papers and provide for everything that is necessary to your client's complete protection, such as *acknowledgment, recording or filing affidavit,* etc.

Note.—Besides statutes and books of forms, see digest and cases on description of property, after acquired property, *mortgagor retaining possession and selling in the course of trade,* the *"insecurity clause,"* *execution,* acknowledgment, affidavit, etc.

CONDITIONAL SALE CONTRACT
Herbert v. Rhodes-Burford Furniture Co.
106 Ill. App. p. 585.

One Belle Harrington, on the 1st of November, 1898, received from appellee a number of articles of furniture, carpets and stoves, and at the time of the receipt of such property she executed to appellee the following contract:

I, Belle Harrington, have received of the Rhodes-Burford Furniture Co. the following described property, * * * which I agree to purchase and pay for as follows: Eight hundred twenty-three and 00/100; $10.00 down and balance payable in installments of $10.00 per week from the date hereof. It is agreed and understood that I may retain the possession of and have use of said goods and chattels until the day the last payment aforesaid becomes due, subject to the conditions hereinafter mentioned.

The title to said property is to remain in said Rhodes-Burford Furniture Co. until fully paid for. And, in event of my failure to promptly pay for the same, as above agreed to, or if I sell, or attempt to sell, or remove property from the said premises hereinafter mentioned, without the written consent of Rhodes-Burford Co., or if at any time they or their assigns shall feel themselves insecure, then the said Rhodes-Burford Furniture Co., their agent, attorneys or assigns, are hereby authorized to take charge of said property with or without force, and may enter any building or room where said goods, or any of them, may be located, and may use all force necessary for the purpose of reclaiming its said goods, even to the extent of breaking locks, doors or windows, if such conduct on its part, or on the part of its attorneys or agents, shall become necessary, and shall sell the same, and out of the proceeds of said sale retain a sufficient amount to pay the balance owing thereon (whether due or not), together with all reasonable costs, charges and expenses in so doing. Said property to be sold at public or private sale to the highest bidder, for cash, after giving ten days' notice posted up in the vicinity where said sale is to take place.

It is understood and agreed that the failure to pay any one of said installments, at the time and in the manner aforesaid, shall make all the installments aforesaid due and payable. And failure of Rhodes-Burford Furniture Co. to take advantage of any default upon my part in making said payments shall in no way operate as a waiver to do so for any subsequent breach. I further agree not to remove said property from Cairo, Ill., until the same is fully paid for, without the written consent of the said Rhodes-Burford Furniture Co.

Witness my hand and seal the 21st day of November, 1898.

(Seal)   (Signed)   Belle Harrington.

This instrument was duly acknowledged before a police magistrate of the city of Cairo on the 22nd of November, 1898;

on the 6th of January, 1899, it was filed for record in the recorder's office of Alexander county.

See Gilbert v. Natl. Cash Reg. Co., 176 Ill. 288.

(Conditional sale, though recorded, not notice and no protection—execution creditor.)

In Illinois, the recording of a contract of conditional sale, acknowledged as a chattel mortgage, of an article allowed to remain in the buyer's possession, affords no protection against a levy thereon by an execution creditor of the buyer or against bona fide purchasers from him.

CHAPTER VIII

PREPARATION OF LEASES AND THEIR PROVISIONS

Protection of Tenant.—A prospective tenant cannot rely entirely upon the ordinary printed forms of leases in renting a house. Printed forms are almost invariably drawn to favor the landlord and to give little or no protection to the interests of the tenant. But although the lessor may request the signature of the lessee to a lease drawn in this manner, it does not follow that the tenant should meekly assent to all of its terms. In the case of taking apartments and offices in large city buildings, a settled form may be demanded and those wishing quarters in the building are sometimes given no option. In most cases, however, the tenant may take a hand in settling the terms of the lease, and should guard himself by some such provisions as are herein suggested, so that he will not be entirely at the mercy of the landlord. He should at least protect himself by a covenant of the lessor to put the lessee into possession of the premises, by a covenant as to the condition of the house or premises, by a covenant to defend the tenant in his possession for the term and by a condition excusing payment of rent in case of damage or destruction of the premises by fire or the elements.

Protection of Landlord.—Is there any reason for the elaborate covenants inserted in leases for the protection of the landlord? Yes, landlords are frequently imposed upon, and the common law has not worked out satisfactorily the rights and liabilities of landlord and tenant, although statutes improve the law somewhat. It is particularly necessary to draft important leases with great care and detail. Every well-drawn lease contains a provision for the forfeiture of the right of possession in case the tenant fails to pay rent, commits waste, or violates his agreements. Provision should also be made as to the rights of the landlord to re-let in case the tenant abandons the premises; also as to repairs to be made by the tenant.

Contract for Lease.—There is a difference between a lease and an agreement for a lease. A contract for a future lease does not give the prospective tenant a right to the premises but only binds the parties to execute a lease according to the agreed terms. If, however, possession is taken, the position of the tenant is much the same as if the agreed lease had been signed.

Formalities.—The Statute of Frauds requires some leases to be in writing. A lease for more than one year is usually required by statute to be in writing and signed by the parties to be charged. Long leases should be executed under seal and should be acknowledged and recorded for the protection of the tenant. Leases should be drawn in duplicate, signed by both parties, and each party should keep one of the copies.

Contents and Provisions of Residence Lease.—The following are some of the matters to be considered in drawing an ordinary lease of a house for purposes of residence:

1. Date and parties, indicating who is lessor and who is tenant. Joinder of lessor's wife in long lease;

2. Explanatory recitals;

3. Operative words that the lessor leases and demises the premises to the tenant at a certain rent;

4. Description of the land leased;

5. The exceptions or reservations, if any;

6. *Habendum,* stating the term or period of the lease; (name the exact date from which the term begins and the period for which it is to run);

7. *Reddendum,* stating the amount of the rent and the time and place of payment;

8. Tenant's covenants:

    (a) To pay the rent promptly as aforesaid; also, perhaps, the insurance and taxes, in a long lease;

    (b) To keep the premises in repair during the term; replace glass broken;

    (c) To permit the lessor to enter and inspect the condition of the premises and make repairs if needed;

    (d) To yield up possession at the end of the term in good repair, except for wear and damage by fire or the elements;

    (e) Covenant against assignment or subletting without the consent of the lessor in writing;

    (f) To maintain gardens and lawn in proper condition; not to cut trees or shrubs;

    (g) Covenant to use as a dwelling only; not to take lodgers;

    (h) Not to make alterations without lessor's approval;

    (i) Not to keep dogs or chickens.

9. Condition of re-entry on non-payment of rent or other breach of covenant; use of force if necessary;

10. Covenant by the lessor to put the lessee in possession. (If the lessee is kept out by some prior tenant unlawfully holding over, the covenant for quiet enjoyment will not protect him from such act of a wrongdoer.)

11. Condition that if the building is destroyed or

injured so as to be untenantable, the lessee may surrender possession and escape further liability for rent. (Option to determine lease at election of either party.).

12. Lessor's covenant for quiet enjoyment, for repairs, external and internal, if so agreed;

13. Lessor's covenant as to the tenantable condition of the premises at the time of letting;

14. Option for renewal of lease and possibly for purchase of fee;

15. Power of landlord to relet in case of abandonment by tenant, without surrender;

16. Surety for payment of rent by lessee.

Business Lease.—Leases of buildings or parts of buildings, for office, commercial and manufacturing purposes often contain very elaborate covenants and provisions. Among these may be mentioned covenants,

1. To keep and obey all statutes, ordinances and sanitary regulations applicable to the premises;

2. To observe all reasonable regulations imposed by insurance companies and not to do anything to increase the rate of insurance;

3. Not to permit inflammable or dangerous material to accumulate on the premises;

4. To keep the premises in a clean and wholesome condition and to remove all ashes and rubbish promptly;

5. That the term shall end at the option of the landlord in case of bankruptcy of the tenant;

6. To indemnify the lessor against liability for damage to other tenants or for open coal holes, slippery walks, etc.;

7. That the lessor shall not be liable for any damages by failure to keep the premises in repair, or from plumbing, gas, water, stream or other pipes leaking or bursting;

8. That the lessee shall be responsible not only for his own acts, but also for those of his family, servants, employees, guests, visitors and lodgers;

9. Provision for termination of the lease in whole or in part from the time when the possession of the whole or part shall be required for public use; the rents to be apportioned;

10. Purchase of the fixtures by the lessor at the end of the lease at a valuation.

Guaranty of Tenant.—It is not uncommon to require of a tenant in the case of a long lease a covenant by a surety somewhat as follows:

John Doe hereby covenants with the lessor in consideration of one dollar, the receipt of which is hereby acknowledged, that the tenant shall at all times during the continuance of this lease pay the rent hereby reserved and perform the covenants herein contained on his part to be performed.

Witness my hand and seal.

(Signed) John Doe. (Seal)

Warranty of Condition.—In a lease of a furnished house there is an implied condition or covenant that it is at the time of letting reasonably fit for habitation, but not that it shall continue so during the whole letting. There is no implied warranty of condition as to an unfurnished house, but only for concealed defects known to the landlord and not disclosed. (Kurtz v. Pauly, 158 Wis. 534.)

Repairs.—A covenant to keep the premises in good repair imposes an obligation on the party making the covenant to put in repair premises which at the time of the demising were not in repair. Under a general covenant to repair without exception, the lessee is liable to rebuild a house which may be destroyed by fire, tempest, lightning, earthquake, or other accident. It is accordingly necessary that an exception should be inserted in the covenant for repairs, as to reasonable wear and tear, and also as to damage by fire or the elements. (See Tiffany, Landlord and Tenant, p. 758.)

Effect of Damage or Destruction.—In case of the damage or destruction of a building leased, the tenant will be bound to pay the rent unless protected by provision in the lease. He will have to continue to pay full rent for the burned out plot of ground, even though he leased highly improved property. This, however, is not the case as to the lease of rooms, offices or apartments which are not regarded as giving any possession of the ground itself, and where the complete destruction of the subject matter excuses rent. In building leases, however, the tenant should protect himself by a provision that in case the building is rendered unfit for the use intended by fire or other accident, then the lease shall either terminate, or at least rent shall be suspended during necessary repairs or rebuilding. Such a provision might be as follows:

"If the whole or any substantial part of the demised premises be destroyed or made unfit for occupancy or use by fire, the elements, inherent defect, or other accident, the lessee having exercised ordinary care as to such injury, shall be entitled to a complete or proportionate abatement of the rent afterwards accruing. He shall not have the right to quit or surrender possession, or terminate the lease except for such an injury as shall render the demised premises substantially unfit for the purposes of the lease."

Liability for Accidental Injuries.—The landlord should be warned as to the dangers of entering into a covenant for repairs. Such a covenant may subject him to liability to the tenant or others for damages resulting from a defective condition of the premises.

Entry.—It is not always understood that the landlord has no right to enter the leased premises to inspect their condition, or for any other purpose, except by consent of the tenant; and is as much a trespasser as a stranger if he enters without license. A provision is accordingly often employed giving the landlord a right to enter to view the condition of the premises or even to make needed repairs and alterations.

Assignment and Subletting.—The tenant may assign or sublet his rights under the lease without the landlord's consent, unless the lease provides otherwise. The object of a covenant against assignment or subletting is to protect the landlord against occupation by an unreliable or irresponsible tenant. The clause against assigning or subletting without the written consent of the landlord is often qualified by provision that the consent shall not be arbitrarily refused. A provision may also be employed providing that the assignee shall at the time of the assignment execute and deliver to the lessor a written instrument agreeing to pay the rent reserved in the lease, and to perform all the conditions and covenants thereof. An assignment will not release the lessee, but he will remain personally liable along with the assignee.

Forfeiture and Re-entry.—A proviso is inserted in every well-drawn lease for the forfeiture of the right to possession and termination of the lease in case the tenant fails to pay rent, commits waste or violates his covenants. A mere breach of covenants does not work a forfeiture or give a right of re-entry at common law. Statutes, however, have been enacted in most jurisdictions providing that, if the lessee fails to pay rent, or fails or neglects to perform the covenants of the lease, the lessor may terminate the lease and recover possession upon certain notice. A landlord who with knowledge of the breach of conditions of a lease for which he has a right of re-entry, receives rent which accrues subsequently, waives the breach and cannot afterwards insist on the forfeiture.

A form of a power to declare forfeiture and re-enter, using force if need be, is taken from the case of *Johnson v. Feilchenfeld* (191 Ill. App., p. 168 at page 170).

RE-ENTRY CLAUSE

"It is expressly agreed between the parties that, if default be made in the payment of the rent above reserved or any part thereof, or in any of the covenants and agreements herein contained, to be kept by the second party, it shall be lawful for the first party at any time thereafter, at the election of said first party, without notice, to declare said term ended; and to re-enter said demised premises or any part thereof, either with or without process of law, and the said second party, or any person or persons occupying the same, to expel, remove and put out, using such force as may be necessary so to do; and the said premises again to repossess and enjoy, as before this demise, without prejudice to any remedies which might otherwise be used for arrears of rent or preceding breach of covenants. * * * And in order to enforce a forfeiture for non-payment of rent, it shall not be necessary to make a demand on the same day the rent shall become due, but a failure to pay at the place aforesaid, or a demand and a refusal to pay on the same day, or at any time on any subsequent day, shall be sufficient, and shall be deemed a forfeiture for non-payment of rent; and after such default or forfeiture shall be made, the second party and all persons in possession under him shall be deemed guilty of a forcible detainer of said premises under the statute."

It may be provided that the lessor is not to take advantage of the right of forfeiture until he has served lessee with a notice of breach, requiring the lessee to remedy it if possible, and the lessee has failed to comply within a certain time, such as 10 or 20 days.

Bankruptcy.—It may also be provided that, "if the tenant shall become bankrupt or insolvent, the rent for the entire month in which the tenant becomes insolvent or bankrupt shall immediately fall due and the lease shall terminate at the end of such month." Such a covenant will create an immediate liability at the filing of a petition in bankruptcy.

Rent and Repairs.—The landlord's breach of his covenant to repair does not absolve the tenant from the duty to pay rent, but as long as he occupies he must continue to pay rent. He may, however, abandon the premises without liability for further rent if they become untenantable. A tenant is not relieved of paying the rent unless the landlord has agreed to make repairs and the property has become untenantable by reason of his failure to do so, and under those circumstances the tenant may abandon the property and thereby relieve himself from liability for the rent.

Abandonment.—If a tenant wrongfully abandons the leased premises before the lease has expired, the landlord may give notice to the tenant of his refusal to accept a surrender, and that he will sublet the premises for the unexpired term for the benefit of the lessee to reduce his damages. Some courts hold that notice to the tenant and consent by him to the re-letting are necessary if he is to be held for any loss sustained in re-letting at a lower rent. It is, therefore, advisable expressly to provide that, in case of abandonment by the tenant, the lessor shall be authorized to enter upon the premises and sublet them for a longer or shorter term, and credit the tenant with any rental that may be obtained without working a surrender by operation of law, or releasing the tenant from liability for rent or damages for breach of covenant.

Provisions of Typical Oil Lease.—In a series of articles on The Law of Oil And Gas (18 Michigan Law Review at page 659), Mr. James A. Veasey states that oil operators have found "that permanent success in the business is possible only when the undertaking is founded upon a lease which involves the following considerations: *First,* the payment of a cash bonus to the lessor at the time of the execution of the lease, the amount of this depending upon the prospective value of the land involved, determined by competition among lessees for leases in the particular locality. *Second,* the lease to provide for a royalty payable to the lessor in the event the property is drilled and success attends the operation. On oil the royalty is a share of the production; on gas it is usually a fixed sum for each well where the gas is ˙utilized. *Third,* where geologic indications are especially favorable, or where the land is in the immediate vicinity of producing wells, the operator will sometimes bind himself to the positive obligation to drill a test well. Occasionally this obligation is supplemented by a stipulation for the drilling of additional wells if the test results in production. *Fourth,* this positive obligation to drill, however, is exceptional, the typical lease containing a provision for a fixed term of limited duration, the consequence being that unless production is found within that term the lease expires. *Fifth,* supplementing the provision for a fixed term is a clause by virtue whereof the lessee has the option either to drill a test well or, in lieu thereof, pay a periodical rental within the definite term. Thus, if the obligation to drill or pay rises to the dignity of

an affirmative covenant to do one or the other, a surrender clause is annexed. If not, the unless clause is
employed. In either event the lessee reserves the
option to escape all obligation under the lease, whether
to drill or to pay, when in his judgment the value of
the property no longer justifies either of the alternative
stipulations. *Sixth,* if the affirmative "drill or pay"
clause is employed, a provision for forfeiture in favor
of the lessor for breach of these conditions is usually
added. If, on the other hand, the unless clause is utilized, the lease terminates *ipso facto* upon failure to drill
or, in the alternative, to pay.

"As a result of this situation, the relative rights and
obligations of the lessor and the lessee are directly
adapted to the peculiar conditions under which the in-
dustry must be conducted, if it is to be permanently
prosecuted. By this method the lessee obtains the right
to explore when explorations are justified, and the right
to abandon the enterprise without further liability when
prudence dictates that course. The lessor, on the other
hand, obtains these advantages: A cash consideration
for his lease equivalent to the prospective value of his
lands for oil and gas purposes, although in fact they
may possess no value whatever to the lessee. The lease
terminates within a definite time unless production is
realized. Moreover, he receives a periodical money payment for such portion of the fixed term of his lease as
the instrument, at the option of the lessee, continues in
force."

About 1880 the typical lease of the period contained
these important provisions in substance:

HABENDUM CLAUSE

To have and to hold said lands for the purpose aforesaid
for a period of five years from date and as long thereafter as
oil or gas shall be produced in paying quantities.

"Drill or Pay" Clause

The lessee agrees to complete a well on said lands within one year from date hereof, or in lieu thereof pay the lessor the sum of One Hundred Dollars per annum until the completion of such well: Provided, should the lessee fail or neglect to drill such well or pay such rental as herein provided, the lessor shall have the right to declare this lease forfeited."

The so-called "unless" clause in the oil and gas lease came later into use. Instead of using a "drill or pay" provision qualified by the right to surrender residing in the lessee, the following stipulation was employed:

Provided, however, that this lease shall become null and void and all rights hereunder shall cease and determine unless a well shall be completed on the premises within one year from the date hereof, or unless the lessee shall pay at the rate of $100 per year in advance for each additional year until such well shall be completed.

"Under this provision the lease terminates *ipso facto* upon the failure to drill or pay, without further liability on the part of the lessee for rentals thereafter accruing."

* * *

Requisition for a Lease of a Dwelling

The Adam Bede Company, a corporation, wishes to lease a dwelling house in Chicago for five years to Richard Roe at a rental of $1,200 per year, payable monthly.

1. Lessee is to have a surety, John Doe, for the performance of his covenants.

2. Lessee is to have option of purchase of fee at $15,000, and of renewal of lease, if premises shall not have been sold, at an advance of ten per cent in the rent.

3. Lease to contain provisions as to assignment and subletting.

4. Effect of damage by fire or accidental casualty of any sort.

5. Repairs by tenant of premises.

6. Restrictions on use of premises; residence only.

7. Covenant by lessee against alterations.

8. Condition of re-entry on non-payment of rent or breach of covenant.

9. Covenant by lessor for quiet enjoyment.

10. Covenant by lessee to yield up at end of term in good repair, except for certain causes.

11. Covenant by lessor to keep the property insured for both parties.

12. Covenant by lessee to comply with all ordinances and regulations of the city as to cleaning streets and sidewalks.

13. Covenant of lessee to remove all ashes and rubbish from the premises within one month prior to termination of the lease.

14. Covenant to use care to preserve the premises from injury by fire or otherwise.

15. Landlord reserves power to make alterations or changes in the premises and to exhibit them to prospective tenants or purchasers.

Draw a careful lease containing a guaranty clause and stipulations covering these points and others such as ought to be covered for the protection of both parties under the present unsatisfactory law of landlord and tenant.

Farm Leases and Contracts for Cropping on Shares.— Farms are often rented for a share of the crops. Under a cropping contract by which the possession of the farm remains in the owner, the one furnishing the labor receives his share of the crops in lieu of wages, and is called a "cropper." The contract is not a lease of the land but is a contract of hiring of labor. The ratio of division of crops depends upon the proportion of value of labor contributed as compared with the capital furnished by the landlord and the rental value of the land. (See Farm Contracts, W. C. Tichenor.)

A lease may also be made upon shares and the line between a cropper's contract and a lease on shares is not always easy to draw. The reasons favoring a share tenancy over a cash rental are as follows:

1. The landlord helps in the management and takes more interest.

2. Tenants may not be willing to pay an absolute cash rental, and the risk to the tenant may be less.

3. The landlord may share in extra profits.

The reasons for cash tenancy are as follows:

1. Cash rent is less bother and there is less chance for controversy.

2. The landlord knows what to expect and does not share the risk of loss of poor seasons and bad management.

3. The tenant prefers to be independent and wants the extra product of good seasons.

4. Cash tenancy pays a good tenant better.

Requisition for Farm Lease

The principal points to be covered in a farm lease from John Doe to Richard Roe are as follows:

1. Parties, who may be described as "landlord and tenant" or "lessor and tenant."

2. The demise or leasing clause.

3. The description of the property, with easements over adjacent land if necessary to the tenant.

4. Reservation of easements, such as rights of way, to the landlord.

5. Habendum: "to the lessee for the term of ...... years from the ...... day of ...., 1920."

6. The amount of rent or share of produce.

7. Items of removable equipment to be furnished by the landlord, referring to an inventory attached.

8. Provisions as to soil management and cropping system to be used.

9. Kinds and amount of live stock to be kept by the tenant.

10. Repairs to be made.

11. Customary restrictions on use of premises.

12. Option to renew or to purchase.

13. Rental a lien on crops grown on the premises and on fixtures.

14. Proviso for declaration of forfeiture and forcible entry.

15. Provision against assignment and underletting.

REQUISITION FOR FARM CONTRACT FOR CROPPING ON SHARES

1. Richard Roe, Cropper, agrees to till and farm for John Doe during one or more farming seasons, the described land in good and husbandlike manner.

2. Cropper to sow and plant and cultivate as owner may direct.

3. Cropper to furnish seed, proper tools and machinery and hired help; and to farm according to his best skill; to keep up fences and gaps to protect crops, fruit, shrubbery and vines; to commit no waste; to harvest, thresh and secure crops; to repair buildings; to cut all weeds before they go to seed.

4. Title to crops to remain in owner.

5. Cropper shall receive one-half or one-third of all the crops in lieu of his wages for labor and care of the place. The rights of Roe shall be those of a cropper. The possession of said farm and all crops shall be in the owner until division.[1]

---

[1] A farm contract or lease may contain provisions as to methods of plowing, planting and cultivation; as to scattering of all manure made on the premises; as to keeping ditches and watercourses clear of obstruction; as to forfeiture if tenant neglects crops; as to cutting of standing timber and so forth.

CHAPTER IX

PREPARATION OF BUILDING AND CONSTRUCTION CONTRACTS

Dangers.—Building and construction contracts are among the most difficult to prepare owing to the detail and complexity of the transaction and dangers arising from the mechanics' lien laws. Owners of land are very much at the mercy of building contractors, and the only safety lies in doing business with the most reliable and responsible persons. A dishonest and unreliable contractor may not only supply a defective structure, but may involve the owner in disastrous litigation with subcontractors, laborers and material-men over liens on the building.

Architect or Engineer.—Prudence dictates that important building or construction contracts be hedged about with many precautions and safeguards for the protection of the owner and employer. In drawing the contract the owner will need in the first place the expert advice of an architect or engineer who knows what should be called for in the way of work and materials. The plans and specifications are of course to be referred to and incorporated as a part of the contract, with provision for alterations, which may increase or decrease the cost.

Supervision.—The owner cannot tell whether he is getting the workmanship and materials which the contractor has agreed to furnish unless these are checked up by the trained professional judgment of an architect or expert builder, exercising direct supervision of the work as it progresses towards completion. Building and construction contracts usually contain stipulations that the work shall be done to the satisfaction of the architect or engineer of the owner, who shall be the sole judge of the quantity, quality and value of material and work furnished and of the interpretation of the plans, drawings and specifications. It is usually provided that the contractor shall not be entitled to recover the various installments of the contract price except on the production of the architect's certificate that the work has been satisfactorily completed.

Certificate.—An architect or engineer, although employed and paid by one of the parties, is treated in this class of contracts as being a kind of umpire or arbitrator, and his certificate as to the quantity, quality and value of the work and the meaning and construction of the specifications can only be attacked for fraud or for errors so gross as to indicate bad faith. In some jurisdictions, however, it is sufficient to show that the certificate has been arbitrarily or unreasonably refused to excuse its production. An arbitration clause that if claims are not approved they shall be determined by arbitration, may operate to relieve the contractor somewhat from the strict requirements of the ordinary certificate provision.

The price is ordinarily made payable in installments according to the progress of the work upon certificate of the architect, and some percentage of the contract price, such as 15 to 25 per cent, is withheld as security until the time for filing mechanics' liens has expired.

It is usual also to require a bond of an individual or surety company to insure faithful performance of the contract by the builder and to protect the owner against mechanics' liens.

The owner may be compelled to pay more than the contract price, if he pays the contractor without requiring statements of amounts due for labor and materials, and the contractor fails to settle with sub-contractors and material-men entitled to liens. Under the mechanics' lien laws of many states the owner is liable to sub-contractors without regard to the contract price or the sum that the owner may be indebted to the contractor.

Power may be given to the architect by written notice to require the dismissal of workmen whom he deems incompetent or careless. A warranty may be exacted, to survive the completion and acceptance of the building, to make good defects arising from improper materials or workmanship which may appear within a period of twelve months.

The American Institute of Architects has recommended standard forms of contracts for owners and builders; also forms of invitations to bid, proposals by builders, surety bonds and general conditions of building contracts. These have been drawn with the view of making them clear and just between owner and contractor. (See Tiffany, Legal Business Forms, pp. 261, 285, Blake on Law of Architecture and Building, App. B.)

The American Railway Engineering Association has provided a general contract form, referring to specifications for each class of work, which in turn may be supplemented by plans or drawings. It has been carefully worked out as a standard for public work or for important corporation construction work. A discussion of the important clauses in such contracts may be found in G. Frank Allen's Business Law for Engineers, Chap. XVI.

For English forms of building contract see I. Key and Elphinstone, Precedents in Conveyancing (10th ed.) p. 1.

For different schemes of arranging the fire insurance on the building during construction, see Tiffany, Legal and Business Forms, pp. 297, 311.

OUTLINE OF PROVISIONS OF BUILDING CONTRACT

1. The contractor agrees to provide all the materials and to perform all the work required to erect the building shown on the plans, specifications and drawings which are attached hereto and made a part of this contract. (The owner may, of course, agree to supply the materials.)

2. Date of commencement of work and time for completion, free of all liens, claims and charges.

3. Provision for so much per day as liquidated damages for delay. Time shall be the essence of the contract.

4. Provisions excusing the contractor for delays caused by frost or inclement weather, or by general strikes of workmen, or in case of alterations or additions requiring additional time.

5. The contract price to be paid on monthly estimates by the architect, less 15 per cent, which reserved amount shall be paid when the contract is completed and the architect satisfied that the building is free from all liens.

6. Alterations and additions may be directed by the architect. These must be ordered in writing. The cost is to be deducted from or added to the contract price; but no bill for extra work shall be allowed unless on certificate or order from owner, countersigned by architect.

7. The contractor admits that the drawings and specifications are sufficient, and covenants to follow them and to furnish all materials of the quality and kind set forth and to execute all work strictly in accord-

ance with the drawings, and to make the work shown and described a perfect and finished job of its kind.

8. In case the parties cannot agree as to the true value of extra or deducted work, or the amount of extra time, or in case they disagree as to the true meaning of any covenant or agreement herein, the decision of the architect shall in each case be final and binding on both.

9. The owner shall insure the buildings and all materials, except tools and appliances, "for and on account of whom it may concern, upon their joint and several interest in the building and materials." (Tiffany Forms, pp. 279, 297.)

10. The owner may upon breach of the building contract settle claims of subcontractors and material-men for which liens could be established, without requiring their establishment, and look to the contractor for reimbursement.

11. The contractor agrees to take all proper precautions against accident or injury to any person, and to be solely responsible for such accidents or injuries, it being agreed that the work shall be done entirely under the control of the contractor, except insofar as provision is made for instructions and supervision by the architect.

12. The contractor is to take down and remove materials and work disapproved by the architect and to make good all work and materials damaged thereby.

13. Contractor to furnish surety company's bond in amount equal to the contract price, conditioned for the faithful performance of the contract and the full payment of all legal claims for labor and material furnished, and for the protection of the owner against all liability or damage of any kind caused by the contractor or his employees in and about the completion of the contract.

14. Owner's right to terminate contract if contractor becomes a bankrupt, or if he persistently or repeatedly refuses or fails to supply enough workmen or proper materials, or if he fails to make prompt payment to subcontractors or material-men, or persistently disregards the instructions of the architect or is guilty of a substantial violation of any of the provisions of the contract.

15. Owner to have right to complete the building upon the contractor's default.

Requisition for Building Contract.—John Doe, the owner, employs Richard Roe, the builder, to erect a dwelling house to cost $10,000 within six months from date, under the supervision of William Smith, architect, and according to plans and specifications drawn by him. The contract is to contain the usual provisions to protect both contractor and owner, particularly against mechanics' liens, but not by waiver of liens. Payments are to be made as the work progresses upon certificate of the architect. Insert the more usual and necessary provisions as to retention of balance, extras, delays and accidents, etc.

FORM OF CONTRACT FOR BUILDING A DWELLING HOUSE AT COST PLUS PERCENTAGE, WHERE OWNER SUPPLIES MATERIALS AND NO ARCHITECT IS EMPLOYED.

This Agreement is made this .... day of ...., 19......, between (hereinafter called the owner) of the one part and .... (hereinafter called the builder) of the other part.

It is agreed as follows:

1. The builder will erect and build for the owner on the owner's land, situate at, etc., and at the spot

indicated on the plan, hereunto annexed, a dwelling-house, and garage, in a substantial and workmanlike manner and in all respects to the satisfaction of the owner. The builder will supply all necessary labor and tools (but not the materials) for the purpose, and at the least cost possible. Such buildings to be completed in all respects according to the drawings, specifications and plans hereunto annexed.

2. The builder will completely finish the said dwelling-house for occupation, and the said garage fit for use, and remove all rubbish from the premises on or before the .... day of .... next (or within .... months from the date on which he commences building), unless prevented by accidents, the elements, strikes, or additions, or alterations ordered by the owner in writing (or other reasonable cause). The building while in process of construction shall be at the risk of the owner as to fire or accidental damage or destruction. The said premises shall be kept free and clear of all mechanics' liens.

3. The owner will pay the builder (weekly) during the progress of the said buildings and works the actual necessary cost of the labor performed in the proper erection of such buildings, as shown by the books of the builder; and in addition thereto a commission at the rate of 10 per cent. of such cost, which shall constitute the builder's profit.

4. The owner will, at his own cost and expense, provide at convenient places near the said site all materials whatsoever necessary for the erection and completion of the said dwelling-house, etc., and pay all expenses of the carriage thereof, and will obtain the necessary permits for said buildings and works. The builder shall be responsible for all materials delivered by the owner on the premises and shall be charged

with any deficiency between the amount delivered and the amount actually used in building and not returned, but all usual allowances for waste shall be made.

5. If the owner shall require any deviation from the said plans and specifications or any more or other buildings or works to be done than those described therein the builder shall consent to such deviations.

6. If the builder shall fail to pay his laborers promptly from week to week, or permit mechanics' liens to be filed, become insolvent, bankrupt, or execute an assignment for the benefit of creditors, or otherwise become unable or fail to carry on the work properly, or if without the written consent of the owner he shall assign or sublet this contract, the owner may by notice in writing sent by registered letter to the builder or left on the site of the said buildings thereupon terminate this contract, and all claim of the builder under this contract shall thereupon cease.

7. If the builder shall in any manner delay or neglect completely to finish the said dwelling-house and buildings, within the times prescribed for the purpose as aforesaid, it shall be lawful for the owner by such notice as aforesaid to require the builder to proceed with such works and on his failing to do so accordingly to employ any other builder to continue and complete the said dwelling-house, and buildings, according to the said plans and specifications, or alterations thereof, and authorize him to use any plant, materials and property of the builder, who shall in such case forfeit all his interest whatsoever under this contract.

8. In case any dispute or difference shall arise between the parties touching or relating either to the said buildings or works, or labor, or cost thereof, or to any other matter or thing arising under this contract, the same, and every of them, shall be referred to (archi-

tect) of etc., or him failing to (architect) of etc., who alone shall consider, value, and determine the same, and whose certificate or award shall be binding and conclusive upon both the said parties.

In witness, etc.,

. . . .
. . . .

(Signatures of both parties)

CHAPTER X

THE PREPARATION OF ARTICLES OF PARTNERSHIP

Dangers of Partnership.—There are certain dangers and disadvantages which are incident to doing business as a partnership. In the first place, in the ordinary partnership, each partner is personally liable for the entire contracts and debts of the firm as well as for his proportionate part of the capital invested. In the second place, each partner is bound by the acts of every other member of the firm within the scope of the firm business, as each partner is agent for the partnership. In the third place, death, bankruptcy, or the sale of one partner's interest in the firm dissolves the firm and the business must be wound up. These disadvantages usually lead business men to conduct business of any considerable size in corporate form, or by some other method than by an ordinary partnership.

The *advantages* of a partnership are these: (1) That it may be formed without expense, simply by contract, either written or oral; (2) That a partnership is free from special corporation taxes and reports, and that there is more elasticity in the organization. Partners, as between themselves, may agree as to any method of dividing liabilities and losses which may be incurred, but this will not protect them against third parties. The Uniform Partnership Act and similar acts which have been adopted in various states, authorize the formation of limited partnerships. In this form the general partners conduct the business and are liable for all the debts, but the special partner is not liable beyond the sum which he contributes to the firm's capital.

Artificial Name.—In some states the transaction of business under a fictitious name, or one using the designation "and company" without filing a certificate setting forth the true names of the partners, is prohibited, and until compliance one may be precluded from enforcing payment for goods sold. (Hunter v. Patterson, 162 Ky. 778, L. R. A. 1915D, 988; Sagal v. Fylar, 89 Conn. 293, L. R. A. 1915E, 747.)

Interest.—Articles of partnership may well be so drawn as to be a code of directions to which the partners may refer as a guide in their transactions. The articles should provide for the payment of interest at a certain rate to each partner on his share of the capital before any division of profits. No such interest will be allowed in the absence of agreement. This provision is important where the contributions of partners are not of equal shares.

Death.—In order that the business shall not have to be wound up, it may be provided that the death of one of the partners shall not cause a dissolution of the firm as to the surviving partners, but that they shall continue the business and shall have the privilege to purchase the interest of the deceased partner at a certain price or at a valuation.

If the surviving members of a partnership continue the trade or business with the partnership stock after the death of a partner, it is at their own risk and they will be liable to account for profits and to bear all losses. No notice of dissolution is necessary to discharge the estate of a deceased partner from liability for any subsequent transaction.

Provision in Will.—A testator may provide in his will for the continuance of his interest in the business so that his whole estate shall be liable for debts which may be incurred. The executor or administrator will also be personally liable if he participates in the partnership business without testamentary authority. [See note, Individual liability of testamentary trustee of business for estate, 40 L. R. A. (N. S.) 202.]

Winding Up.—The surviving members of a firm have authority to wind up a partnership, and the executor or representative of the deceased partner has no right to control the survivors but merely a right to an accounting. The winding up of the affairs consists in selling the property, receiving money due the firm, paying the firm debts and the advances of partners, returning the contributed capital and dividing the profits.

The continuance of the business of a partnership by the executor of a deceased partner involves a new partnership with partnership liability. As Carter, C. J., says in Andrews v. Stinson (254 Ill., pp. 111-124):

"Where there are provisions in the articles of agreement or will for the continuance of the business after the death of one of the partners, it is sometimes inaccurately said that the death of the partner does not dissolve the partnership. If the business is carried on after the death of the partner under such arrangement or by the agreement of the heirs or personal representatives of the deceased, there is, in effect and in law, a new partnership, of which the survivors and the executors or heirs are the members, the new members becoming liable, as the old, to the creditors of the firm."

Outline of Provisions of Partnership Articles

Articles of partnership should define the purposes and time for which the partners associate themselves together in business, and indicate how they are to share profits and losses and conduct the business generally. Matters which may well be provided for are as follows:

1. The members, the nature of the business, the firm name and the place of business.

2. The time of commencement and duration of the partnership, which may be dissolved at will by any partner if the term of existence is not stipulated.

3. The capital: proportions in which it is to be contributed in cash and property; when to be paid; shares in which it is to belong to and to be credited on the books of the firm to each partner.

4. Shares in profits and losses, which will be equal, unless otherwise agreed.

5. The rate of interest to be paid on capital contributions, if any.

6. How books of account shall be kept.

7. Annual accounting.

8. Bank account and authority to sign checks.

9. Withdrawals of so much per month by each partner, provided this does not exceed a certain percentage of his probable share of profits.

10. Time and attention to be given to the business. Vacations.

11. Prohibition against engaging in other business, against speculation and becoming surety for another.

12. Disposition of shares of deceased or retiring partners.

13. Dissolution and methods of winding up.

14. Power of expulsion for misconduct.

15. Provision for continuance of business in case of death or assignment of one of the partners.

16. Limitations on the authority of the partners to bind the firm, as that no clerk or other employee shall

be engaged or discharged save by a majority; and no salary or wages shall be increased save by mutual agreement.

17. That in event of dissolution the partnership affairs shall be settled under the direction of some reputable certified public accountant.

18. That if any partner shall not pay his indebtedness to the firm within 60 days after it is due, or shall violate the terms of this contract in any material respect, or shall fail to account to the firm for moneys received, this partnership shall be dissolved on 30 days' notice.

19. That each partner shall enter in the books all receipts, charges, and withdrawals with necessary particulars.

Limited Partnership.—The lawyer is sometimes called upon to devise an arrangement by which one man can loan capital to a business and share in its profits and yet avoid the liability of a partner for the debts of the business. This may be conveniently accomplished by a limited partnership, which differs from an ordinary partnership in that the business is carried on by the general partner or partners alone, to the exclusion of any limited partner, who must not take part in the management.

The limited partner is not liable for the debts and obligations of the firm, and only the general partners are so liable. The limited partner risks only the capital contributed by him to the partnership, which he cannot withdraw during the continuance of the partnership. A limited partnership is formed under the Uniform Limited Partnership Act, when two or more persons desiring to form a limited partnership, shall sign, swear to and file for record in the office of the recorder of deeds where the principal office of the limited partnership is located, a certificate which shall state the agreement as to the following points:

I. The name of the partnership;

II. The character of the business;

III. The location of the principal place of business;

IV. The name and place of residence of each member; general and limited partners being respectively designated;

V. The term for which the partnership is to exist;

VI. The amount of cash and a description of and the agreed value of the other property contributed by each limited partner;

VII. The additional contributions, if any, agreed to be made by each limited partner and the times at which or events on the happening of which they shall be made;

VIII. The time, if agreed upon, when the contribution of each limited partner is to be returned;

IX. The share of the profits or the other compensation by way of income which each limited partner shall receive by reason of his contribution;

X. The right, if given, of a limited partner to substitute an assignee as contributor in his place, and the terms and conditions of the substitution;

XI. The right, if given, of the partners to admit additional limited partners;

XII. The right, if given, of one or more of the limited partners to priority over other limited partners, as to contributions or as to compensation by way of income, and the nature of such priority;

XIII. The right, if given, of the remaining general partner or partners to continue the business on the death, retirement or insanity of a general partner, and

XIV. The right, if given, of a limited partner to

demand and receive property other than cash in return for his contribution.

The Uniform Limited Partnership Act provides that "A limited partnership may carry on any business which a partnership without limited partners may carry on, except banking, insurance, brokerage and the operation of the railroads.

"The contributions of a limited partner may be cash or other property, but not services.

"The surname of a limited partner shall not appear in the partnership name, unless (a) it is also the surname of a general partner, or (b) prior to the time when the limited partner became such the business had been carried on under a name in which his surname appeared.

(2) "A limited partner whose name appears in a partnership name contrary to the provisions of paragraph (1), is liable as a general partner to partnership creditors who extend credit to the partnership without actual knowledge that he is not a general partner."

"A limited partner shall not become liable as a general partner unless, in addition to the exercise of his rights and powers as a limited partner, he takes part in the control of the business."

REQUISITION FOR ARTICLES OR CERTIFICATE OF ORGANIZATION OF LIMITED PARTNERSHIP

Prepare articles or certificate of organization of a limited partnership, in which Baker P. Andrews shall be a limited partner. The following points are to be covered, and others which may occur to you.

1. The name of the partnership shall be Stinson & Hand.

2. The character of the business shall be that of the

retail lumber business to be carried on at Summerdale in Chicago, which shall be the principal place of business.

3. The names and residence of the members are as follows: Baker P. Andrews, Lincoln, Illinois; (limited partner). Archibald J. Stinson, Chicago, Illinois, (general partner). Nelson T. Hand, Chicago, Illinois, (general partner).

4. The term for which the partnership is to exist is three years.

5. The capital of the firm shall be $80,000, of which sum said Andrews is to furnish one-half and the two other partners one-fourth each.

6. Provisions for additional contributions and for payment or return to the limited partner at the conclusion of the business.

7. Share of profits or income, one-third each.

8. Provision that new limited partners may be added.

9. Priority of claim and 6% per annum on the contribution of the limited partner on dissolution.

10. Right to continue business on the death or retirement of the limited partner.

11. Right to receive property other than cash in return for contributions of capital.

12. Control of the business.

13. Partnership books.

14. Renewal of partnership agreement.

15. Dissolution.

16. Execution, affidavits, and filing for record.

CHAPTER XI

THE ORGANIZATION OF CORPORATIONS AND ISSUE OF SECURITIES

Incorporation.—It is often a question whether or not to incorporate. The expense and trouble of incorporation may not be advisable, as the business may be carried on better in some other way. The next question is where to incorporate. Domestic incorporation is usually preferable. Foreign incorporation fees are wasted if one has to pay the same fees for the privilege of conducting business in the home state.

The various steps usually required to create a corporation ready for business under modern statutes may be enumerated as follows:

1. Drafting of the articles of incorporation;
2. The signing and sometimes sealing of the articles by the requisite number of incorporators, and acknowledgment of the same before a notary public;
3. The filing and recording the articles with the Secretary of State and the payment of the organization tax and fees;
4. The filing of a copy of the articles duly certified with the register of deeds or other county official in the county in which the corporation is domiciled;
5. The organization of the corporation ready for the transaction of business by the issuance and payment of a certain amount of stock and the holding of the first meetings of stockholders and directors;
6. Securing the necessary permit, if any is required, from the Secretary of State for the transaction of busi-

ness as a corporation. [Frost, Incorporation and Organization of Corporations (4th Ed.), pp. 12, 878.]

Articles of Incorporation.—The drafting of the incorporation paper, articles of association or, certificate of incorporation, as it is sometimes called, is a comparatively simple matter. Printed forms of articles are usually furnished by the Secretary of State of the different states free of charge on application. The organization and issue of securities for a large corporation, however, require a high degree of legal skill and experience. The most important and difficult parts of the articles are the object clauses setting forth the purposes for which the corporation is organized. These should be made sufficiently broad to cover the various transactions that may be found convenient in the course of the company's business, and at the same time exclude business which is not contemplated. [Machen, Modern Law of Corporations, Sec. 46-108; Palmer's Company Law (9th ed.), pp. 64, 65.]

In a few states (Arizona, California, Delaware, Iowa, Kentucky, and Utah) if it is desired to protect stockholders from personal liability for corporate debts, a provision exempting stockholders from such liability must be inserted in the articles. Some states require that the articles shall contain a statement as to the amount of stock subscribed, the amount of capital stock paid in, the names of the first board of directors, and the date of the annual meeting.

The personal element in the management of a corporation may be important for the sake of secrecy and the protection of stockholders. A provision to guard the membership may be made in the articles of incorporation requiring stockholders to give the corporation the privilege or option of purchasing stock which may be offered for sale by terms somewhat as follows: "If at any time any of the stockholders or subscribers hereto, or their assigns, desire to sell and dispose of their stock, they shall first offer it in writing to the board of directors, stating price and terms, and give the directors ten days in which to place it with the other stockholders. At the expiration of ten days they shall have the right to sell to outsiders upon the same terms and at the same price." (Casper v. Kalt-Zimmers Manufacturing Co., 159 Wis. 517.)

Capitalization.—The basis of capitalization is often actual or hoped for earning capacity rather than tangible assets. In the case of close corporations the capital stock is often issued at a face value much less than the actual value. Future taxation, federal and state, must be carefully considered. The incorporation fee and the annual franchise tax are usually based on the authorized capitalization. A federal stamp tax of five cents on each $100.00 of face value is imposed on each original issue of capital stock.

OUTLINE OF ARTICLES OF INCORPORATION

The articles of incorporation state the agreement as to the essentials of the proposed organization, define and limit its purposes and its capital stock, and should cover all of the matters required by the law of the state of incorporation. These are in general:

1. The names of the incorporators, who may usually be from three to seven in number, who subscribe for one or more shares of stock;

2. The name of the corporation, which should include the word "company," "limited" or "incorporated."

3. The corporate purposes and powers, which should be made sufficiently broad and inclusive to cover all business likely to be undertaken.

4. Capitalization, so many thousand dollars.

5. The number of shares and their par value and classification as common or preferred, and in some states the amount subscribed.

6. The location of the principal office of the company.

7. The duration, which in some states is limited to a certain period of years, but in many may be made perpetual.

8. The number of directors in whom the management of the corporation is to be invested.

9. The names of the first board of directors must sometimes be specified in the articles.

10. Other provisions required or permitted by the law of the particular state, such as exemption from individual liability.

11. Execution and acknowledgment. (See I Machen, Modern Law of Corporations, Sec. 109-126.)

By-Laws.—The by-laws are usually prepared by the attorney in advance of the first meeting for adoption by the stockholders, although in some states they may be adopted by the directors. They should contain a systematic statement of rules for the internal government of the corporation. They will usually provide for such matters of corporate business as the issue and transfer of certificates of stock, the meetings of the stockholders and directors, the election and removal and duties of officers and the method of amendment by majority or two-thirds vote. They may be so drawn as to favor the interests of the majority and enable them to control the corporation, or for the protection of the rights of minority stockholders. They should be carefully drawn, adopted and recorded in the minute book of the corporation. (Clephane, Business Corporations, p. 203.)

Conditions to Doing Business.—Corporations may not as a rule commence business until a certain pro-

portion of the required amount of capital has been paid
in and subscribed. In Wisconsin, for example, 20 per
cent of the par value of one-half the capital stock must
be actually paid in before a corporation can transact
business with others than its members. (La Crosse v.
Goddard, 114 Wis., 610.) Under the 1919 revision of
the Corporation Act of Illinois, "the amount of stock
to be issued at once is to be specified in the articles,
and there is nothing in the statute except the fees, to
prevent the organization of a corporation with an
authorized capital of $1,000,000 and with only $1,000
issued at once, of which only one-half need to be paid
in. The incorporation fee of one-twentieth of one per
cent is based upon the authorized capital." (W. B.
Hale, The New Corporation Act and the Securities
Law, 14 Ill. Law Rev., p. 358.)

First Meetings.—The main business at the first
meeting of stockholders is the election of directors and
the adoption of by-laws.

It is customary to prepare the papers relating to the
first meeting of the stockholders and of the directors
in advance. These minutes should show the giving of
notice, or waiver of notice by the incorporators and
subscribers, the names of those present in person or
by proxy, the adoption of by-laws and the election of
directors. The motions and resolutions recited in the
minutes may be simply read, not actually carried out,
or the parties may actually go through the motions.
There may also be presented at the first meeting of the
stockholders a resolution authorizing the directors to
accept a formal proposition for the issuance of stock in
exchange for property.

The minutes of the first meeting of the directors
will show a call or waiver of notice; a list of those
present; a motion that the secretary shall cast a ballot

for a recited list of officers; the adoption of a form of
stock certificate; a resolution to authorize the secretary to provide a seal, minute book and other corporate books; the acceptance of subscriptions of stock, if
any; and a resolution to accept a proposition for the
exchange of a specified number of shares of stock for
certain property and to authorize the officers to issue
the stock, if this plan is adopted. The meeting may
be adjourned over for a few days to avoid the necessity
of another call.

Issue of Stock as Full Paid.—To issue stock direct
for less than par would leave the purchasers liable to
assessments for the difference. Expedients are therefore utilized to render the common stock full paid before it is sold below par or given as a bonus. The
most convenient device is that referred to by which
the corporation accepts a proposition to issue its stock
in whole or in part, in exchange for real or personal
property, or even in payment for services. [See
Conyngton, Corporate Management. Frost, Incorp.
and Org. of Corps. (4th ed.), pp. 837, 838.]

The purchasers will then assign back to the corporation or to some trustee for the corporation, a proportion of this full paid stock, to be used for corporate
purposes. The stock is usually assigned back to the
corporation itself. This issue of fully paid stock, which
has been donated to or purchased by the company, is
then held subject to disposal by directors and may be
sold below par or given as a bonus with preferred stock
or bonds without liability. In general full paid stock
carries no liabilities of any kind either to the corporation or to its creditors, except in a few states. It is
therefore very desirable in issuing stock for sale to
render the stock full paid and non-assessable.

When full paid stock is issued for property received

there must be actual fraud in the transaction to enable creditors of the corporation to call the stockholders to account. A gross and obvious over-valuation of the property would be evidence of fraud. (Whitehill v. Jacobs, 75 Wis. 474, 119 U. S. 343.)

Requisition for Organization of a Corporation.— Ames is the owner of Blackacre adjoining the city of Madison, which he wishes to lay out in city lots, grade the lots and streets and put the property on the market. For this purpose he wishes to organize a corporation with a capital stock of $50,000. The land cost Ames $15,000 and is subject to a mortgage of $5,000. He proposes to put the land in subject to the mortgage at a valuation of $40,000, to be paid for in stock of the company. Ten thousand dollars' worth of treasury stock is to be donated back to the company. The balance of the stock is to be taken by Bates and Call in equal shares in cash, the cash to be used in developing the property.

You are employed by Ames to prepare complete incorporation papers under the laws of your own state, including articles and by-laws, and also full minutes of the first meetings of stockholders and directors, and to indicate the taking of steps necessary to organize the corporation ready for business and to authorize the issue of the stock for the property. Draw all the necessary papers to make the stock full paid and non-assessable in consideration of the property received, and put $10,000 worth of full paid stock in the corporate treasury. Cite form books, texts and authorities consulted at the end of your paper.

The action taken at the meetings should appear in the minute book, not the arguments or immaterial details. A proper record of the proceedings of every corporation is important and is competent evidence to show the acts of the corporation. Minutes should be signed by the secretary and approved at the next subsequent meeting.

Requisition for Corporation Not for Profit.—A fraternity or social club wishes to incorporate and build a club house. If they can do so, draw the necessary papers under the statutes relating to corporations organized not for profit. Supply additional facts if needed.

REQUISITION FOR INCORPORATION
(The University of Chicago Law School, Practical Exercises in Private Corporations)

Each member of the class will prepare and hand in papers for the organization of a manufacturing or mercantile corporation, as follows:

1. A complete set of incorporation papers duly executed in pursuance of the statutes and with endorsements as to filing, recording, and the like; a set of by-laws; minutes of the meetings of shareholders and directors, showing the complete organization of the corporation, the adoption of the by-laws, the election of officers; and proper resolutions authorizing the issue of common and preferred stock, with a form of each duly executed. Names, descriptions, amounts or other additional data required to carry out the foregoing arrangements will be supplied by the students;

2. The papers will be prepared under the laws of the state in which the student expects to practice, if that be decided upon; otherwise under the laws of Illinois, Delaware, Maine or New Jersey. Blanks in common use may be employed. All written parts will be typewritten. Great care should be taken with the by-laws to see that they constitute a workable and efficient supplement to the Articles or Charter. Atten-

tion should also be given to the accuracy, appropriateness and lawyer-like quality of the phraseology;

3. The papers will be handed in at least one week before the close of the course. They should be endorsed with the name of the student and of the state in which the incorporation is effected, and with a certificate that they are the personal work of the student who submits them. Fasten all securely together under one cover. Do not fold;

4. These papers will be required for credit and will be graded and marked according to their merit. They may, at the student's option, be offered in lieu of any two questions upon the examination, or as two additional questions;

5. The following books will be found helpful:

Clephane on Business Corporations;
Conyngton on Corporate Organization;
Dill on Corporations in New Jersey;
Fletcher on Corporation Forms and Precedents;
Boisot on By-Laws;
Jones' Legal Forms;
Wood's Modern Business Corporations.

6. Do not rely too implicitly upon the forms found, especially in the matter of by-laws. Some of the forms frequently given are not very good. Test your by-laws by various hypothetical situations and see how they would work.

SUGGESTIONS IN REGARD TO SECURITY ISSUES AND CORPORATE REORGANIZATIONS

(Submitted by A. A. Ballantine, of the New York City Bar)

Determination of the Problem.—When an attorney has occasion to pass upon or prepare the papers for an issue of securities such as stock, bonds, debentures or notes, or for corporate reorganizations, he should first carefully determine just what the client desires to have accomplished and what the reasons are for the step which the client proposes to have taken. In the effort to make such a determination, it not infrequently develops that something different should be done than that which the client contemplates. The attorney should endeavor to get clearly in mind the business aspects of the problem, as the whole purpose of the financing or reorganization papers is to accomplish a certain business object, in the light of which the papers are to be prepared.

Statement of the Plan.—After the problem has been carefully ascertained, there should then be prepared a statement of the plan. This should recite that the corporation (or corporations) in question are organized under the laws of a certain state (or states) giving dates of organization; should recite their outstanding capitalization; should also in most cases recite or refer to their most recent balance sheets and perhaps to their income accounts for one or more years. It should then recite that it is proposed to issue new capital as follows, or merge or consolidate the corporations into a new corporation which shall have the following capitalization. It should then recite how the new securities are to be handled, setting forth what are to go to old security holders, what are to be taken by the bankers and the consideration which is to be paid and received in each case.

Legal points to be borne particularly in mind in preparing the plan and the papers to carry it out, are as follows:

Authorization for Issue of Securities.—Where new securities are to be issued, the legal authority for their issue is, of course, to be found primarily in the statutes of the state under which the corporation is created. These should, of course, be consulted, making sure to consult the latest statutes of the state. There should also be considered whether the new securities require approval by any administrative officer of the state, such as a Commissioner of Corporations, or a Secretary of State, or by any state board such as a Board of Public Utilities. It should be borne in mind that under the present laws of some states, approval by a Board is sometimes required even in the case of corporations which are not of a public service character, as for example in the case of the merger of certain corporations in New Jersey. After the statutes have been consulted a list should be prepared showing each approval which is required. If the securities are to be sold in a state other than the state of incorporation, there should also be considered the requirements of that state under its Blue Sky or other laws as to the sale of securities so that these requirements can be complied with. If the corporation is to do business in states other than the state of its creation, the requirements of each state in which it is to be licensed to do business should also be considered. It may be found, for example, that a corporation which is to have a stock of no par value cannot be qualified to do business in a state in which it will have to carry on business, as for example, the State of Missouri.

Stock Exchange Requirements.—If the proposed securities are to be listed on any exchange, either presently or in the future, a statement of the listing requirements should be obtained from the secretary of the exchange and a statement prepared showing just what such requirements are and how each requirement is to be met.

Taxation Problem.—Taxation problems are, of course, today of very great importance and must be carefully considered in making up the financing or reorganization plan.

Federal Taxation.—The question should be considered whether the reorganization will involve upon any company any federal tax. Reference should be made to section 201 of the Revenue Act of 1918 and the material Treasury Decisions and Regulations. The questions here involved concern both possible income and excess profit taxes which may result from a sale or transfer involved in a reorganization, and also the determination of the allowable invested *capital* of the reorganized company. These questions are of too great complication to be dealt with in this statement.

State Taxation Questions.—There should also be considered how the new or reorganized company will be taxed within the state of its domicile. If the corporation is to do business in other states, questions of the taxation in those states should also be dealt with.

Use of Corporate Records.—No papers for the issue of new securities or for the reorganization of corporations should be put in final form until the records of each corporation to be dealt with have been carefully examined from the date of its incorporation to make sure as to the legality of all its existing and outstanding securities and just how they have been issued. There should also be an examination made to determine whether the corporation has filed with every state such papers as were required to make lawful any issue, increase or reduction of stock.

Balance Sheet.—Nothing is of more importance in preparing the new papers than the making up at various stages of a new balance sheet of the company or companies as they will appear after the reorganization or new issue has been carried through. This involves careful determination as to just how the issue of the securities is to be handled. The work is not complete unless the opening journal or other entries to be made in the plan to be carried out have been agreed upon by the treasurer or other financial officer of the corporation instructed to make them.

Caution in Preparing of Papers.—Care as to detail is of the utmost importance in preparing satisfactory papers of this character. It is very important to make sure that the same word or phrase is always used in the papers to describe the same thing and is not used in different senses in different connections. The attorney preparing the papers should himself carefully read through every word after they have been written out by the stenographer and should compare and re-read every new draft to make sure that there are no stenographic or other errors. If the client discovers such errors in such papers, it weakens his confidence in all other work.

The attorney should have before him at every stage, a memorandum showing just what is to be accomplished and every paper which is required, the papers being checked off as prepared.

When the final transactions are to be put through, the attorney should have a paper detailing every step which is to be taken so that he can make a check as each step is taken and make sure that nothing is omitted. This paper should show all revenue stamps which are called for, the order in which the steps should be taken, etc.

When the work is completed, the attorney should himself read through in the company's minute books the entire record of the transactions and should also

himself look at the actual entries upon the corporation's books.

PRACTICAL EXERCISE IN CONSOLIDATION OF CORPORATION AND PARTNERSHIP AND ISSUE OF SECURITIES

(The University of Chicago Law School)

Certain persons are promoting the organization of
Union Implement Company, a corporation, to acquire,
take over and continue the several properties and business of Reed, Jones & Spencer (a co-partnership, com-
posed of Edward D. Jones and Ralph K. Spencer),
and the Eclipse Windmill Company, a corporation (of
which Nelson Lambert is President and Arthur P.
Willis is Secretary-Treasurer), all being engaged in the
business of manufacturing and selling various non-
competing varieties of agricultural implements. The
promoters expect to pay for the properties, good-will,
business, etc., which the new company is thus to acquire by the issue and sale of both common and 6%
cumulative preferred stock, and first mortgage 20-year
5% coupon bonds, of Union Implement Company. They
have arranged with a bond house to underwrite this
stock and bond issue when the bond house is satisfied
that the new company has been legally organized, and
has acquired title to the properties in question, and
that the stock and bonds have been lawfully authorized
and issued. The counsel for the bond house require
the following papers:

I. A digest or outline of the constitutional and
statutory rules of the state, respecting private corporations, showing briefly (a) any constitutional provisions
which may affect the proposed corporation, (b) an
outline of the statute under which it is proposed to

organize, showing the requirements of the statute as to form, execution, filing, recording, publishing, payment of fees, date of taking effect, and the like, giving proper citations to the volumes and sections referred to;

II. A complete set of incorporation papers of Union Implement Company, duly executed in pursuance of the statutes and with endorsements as to filing, recording, and the like; a set of by-laws; minutes of the meetings of shareholders and directors, showing the complete organization of the corporation, the adoption of the by-laws and the election of officers;

III. Forms of conveyance from Reed, Jones & Spencer, and the Elipse Windmill Company respectively of all their property, business, good-will, etc., to Union Implement Company; resolutions of the latter company accepting such conveyances, and proper resolutions authorizing the issue and sale of the common and preferred stock and first mortgage bonds as above specified, with a form of each duly executed. An abstract of the provisions of the trust deed securing such bonds will also be provided.

Each member of the class will prepare and hand in the foregoing papers. Names, descriptions, amounts or other additional data required to carry out the foregoing arrangements will be supplied by the student.

The papers will be prepared under the laws of the state in which the student expects to practice, if that be decided upon; otherwise under the laws of Illinois, Delaware, Maine or New Jersey. Blanks in common use may be employed. All written parts will be typewritten. Great care should be taken with the by-laws to see that they constitute a workable and efficient supplement to the Articles or Charter. Attention should also be given to the accuracy, appropriateness and lawyer-like quality of the phraseology.

Voting Trusts.—The object of a voting trust is to assure continuity of management, policy and control of a corporation. The general plan is as follows: A majority of the stockholders transfer their stock in whole or in part into the hands of trustees. The trustees have the transfer registered on the books of the company, and surrender the certificates so assigned, taking in return new certificates in their names as trustees. The trustees issue trust certificates to those in the pool. Dividends are to be paid over to the certificate holder less expenses. By this arrangement the voting power is separated from the beneficial ownership of the stock. [H. A. Cushing, Voting Trusts (1915) II and IV for collection of valuable data, suggestions and precedents for draftsmen of such agreements.]

There has been a great deal of question as to the validity of voting trusts, and in some jurisdictions stockholders cannot irrevocably surrender the voting power of the stock. The points to be guarded against in drafting such an arrangement in order to assure its validity are as follows: (1) The purpose should appear to be for the benefit of the whole body of stockholders; (2) trustees should be selected from among the stockholders; (3) the substitution and appointment of new trustees for the original trustees should be provided for; (4) the agreement should recite valuable consideration and should be sealed; (5) the arrangement should be open to any stockholders who wish to join on deposit of their stock.

The following is a form of voting trust taken in substance from Luthy v. Ream, 190 Ill. App., 315, 317. In the Supreme Court the agreement was held not to be binding, 270 Ill. 170; 279 Ill. 54, 56.

Form of Voting Trust

This agreement made this fourth day of September, 1912, by and between the undersigned (41) stockholders of Peru Plow and Wheel Company and Henry Ream, one of the stockholders of said company, hereinafter referred to as trustee, WITNESSETH:

WHEREAS, The said stockholders deem it to their interest and for the benefit of the whole body of stockholders that all of their stock should be voted as a unit upon all questions affecting the business management of said company and the said Ream has consented to hold and vote such stock on behalf of the stockholders,

It is hereby agreed between the said stockholders and said trustee in consideration of the mutual covenants and agreements herein expressed, the assignment and delivery of certificates of stock to said trustee, pursuant to this agreement of the number of shares of stock of said company set opposite their respective names, that said stock shall be held in trust by the said trustee for the said stockholders by whom it was severally assigned upon the terms and conditions, as follows:

1. The said Trustee shall hold, control and vote said stock as if he was the owner of all of said stock;

2. Said Trustee shall determine how said stock shall be voted upon any question, at any time, and at every meeting of the stockholders;

3. All of said stock so held by the Trustee shall be voted as a unit;

4. At all elections of directors of the Peru Plow and Wheel Company, said Trustee shall nominate three directors, to be voted for at such election, and said Trustee shall vote all said stock held by him as

a unit for each and all of the directors so nominated by him;

5. Any vacancy which may be caused by death, resignation or removal of the trustee, shall be filled by a majority in amount of the persons who then hold the stock now owned by the parties to the agreement;

6. Said Trustee shall prepare and issue to the stockholders certificates showing the amount of stock held on behalf of each stockholder respectively, and the stock so held may be divided and transferred in like manner as if it had not been assigned in trust, subject to the rights and powers of the Trustee under this assignment. But no such assignment, or transfer of stock, shall be effective for any purpose until surrender of the certificate issued by said Trustee, and the issue of a new certificate to the purchaser or assignee thereof;

7. No fee shall be charged by such Trustee herein designated for any services performed in connection with the trust hereby created;

8. Said Trustee shall collect and receive all dividends on the stock transferred to and held by him and shall immediately pay over the same to the holders of trust certificates representing such stock as their respective interests appear. The Trustee shall not demand or receive any compensation for receiving and paying over such dividends;

9. The rights, duties and powers hereby conferred upon said Trustee shall expire and wholly cease on the first day of September, A. D. 1922, and the Trustee shall, at said time, assign and transfer to the persons who then hold Trustee's certificates, evidencing their ownership of shares of stock, the amount of stock to

which each holder thereof is shown by his Trustee's certificate to be entitled;

10. Said Trustee hereby accepts the trust hereby created and hereby undertakes to hold, own and vote said stock as therein provided, and to re-transfer the same on the first day of September, A. D. 1922, to the holders of Trustees certificates, evidencing their right to receive the same;

11. Said Trustee further undertakes at all times to vote the said stock by himself, or by proxy, and exercise his powers as Trustee in such manner as he shall deem to be for the best interests of the stockholders of the Peru Plow and Wheel Company. Said Trustee further undertakes to accept additional assignments of stock from any and all stockholders of the Peru Plow and Wheel Company, and to permit any stockholder thereof to become a subscriber to this agreement;

12. This contract shall continue and shall not be revoked before September 1, 1922.

Henry Ream. (Seal)
Trustee.
Stockholders. (Seal)

No. of Shares

. . . .

CHAPTER XII

BUSINESS TRUSTS AS A SUBSTITUTE FOR CORPORATIONS

Advantages.—The device of creating a business trust as a substitute for a corporation is one that has attracted attention in recent years, particularly in Massachusetts. These are sometimes known as "Massachusetts Trusts," or "common law trusts." They imitate as closely as possible the scheme of corporate organization and seek to obtain most of the advantages incident to corporations, free from the expense, taxation and regulations imposed by law upon corporations. Their advantages are that they furnish a method of co-operative ownership and management of capital, more economical, convenient and flexible than the corporate form. No filing or recording of articles is necessary unless under recent statutes, such as that of Oklahoma. No incorporation tax need be paid. The restrictions upon foreign corporations doing business in a state, requiring them to procure a license and pay various taxes and fees, do not apply to trusts.

The Danger.—The great problem in organizing a business trust is to do business through the trustees, and at the same time avoid creating the relationship of principal and agent, or that of partners on the part of the beneficiaries who have the ultimate ownership of the business.[1] As a general rule if one is proprietor

---

[1] See Wrightington, Unincorporated Associations, pp. 35, 40. 52, 56, 128; Sears, Trust Estates as Business Corporations; Fletcher, Cyclopedia Corporations, Vol. 9, Sec. 6061.

of a business he is personally liable upon its debts and contracts; and if two or more are proprietors there is a joint liability as partners which cannot be avoided at law except by incorporation. It is interesting to observe how closely a business trust can be made to resemble a corporation. Most of the corporate forms can be adapted to the purpose.

Trust Agreement.—In organizing a business trust an agreement and declaration of trust is drawn up covering essential points which are similar to those covered by articles of incorporation. It is drawn between the subscribers, or contributors of the trust property, and the trustees. It designates (1), the trustees and provides for a trust name; (2), it provides for the raising and conveying the trust property or fund to the trustees; (3), it prescribes the rights, powers and duties of the trustees, which in general define the purposes of the trust; (4), it provides for the issue of transferrable certificates or shares to those who are the beneficiaries in proportion to their interest in the property and profits; (5), it provides for the division of profits; (6), it limits the liability of the trustees and beneficiaries to the trust property; (7), it fixes the duration of the trust; (8), it provides for dissolution of the trust and for succession of trustees. (H. L. Wilgus, Corporations and Express Trusts as Business Organizations, 13 Mich. Law Rev. 205, 208; Fletcher, Cyclopedia Corporations, Vol. 9, p. 10477, Sec. 6067.)

Conveyance.—The preamble of the trust agreement designates the parties. It is then recited that certain property is to be conveyed to the trustees, giving a specific description. This conveyance may be made by a separate deed. The trustees declare that they will hold the property so to be transferred, together with other property which they may receive as trustees, in trust to manage, invest and distribute the income thereof to the holders of certificates.

Trust Name.—A trust name is usually adopted, such as "Houghton Building Trust." In some states persons carrying on business under an artificial name must file a certificate giving the real names and addresses of the persons owning and conducting the business, in this case the trustees.

Duration.—It is doubtful whether a trust can be created of indefinite duration without violating the rule against restraints on alienation, unless the trustees have the power to sell at any time. (Hart v. Seymour, 147 Ill. 598, 609.) A trust may in most states be created to continue for a term of 21 years from the death of the last survivor of a list of persons named. Children are often mentioned for this purpose. In some states a different period during which the power of alienation may be suspended by a trust, is prescribed by statute. (Wilgus, 13 Mich. Law Rev. 221.)

Powers.—A declaration of trust will authorize the trustees to engage in one or more lines of business more or less specifically designated. It will give the trustees full control of the trust property, with power to make it answerable for their acts and contracts, in the conduct of the business of the trust. It will also give power to purchase property, to issue shares in payment for it, to execute contracts and to exercise such powers as are possessed by directors of a corporation.

Exemption.—The agreement will provide for the exemption of the trustees from personal liability. It may be provided that "in every written order, contract or obligation which the trustees shall give, authorize, or enter into, it shall be the duty of the trustees to stipulate that neither the trustees nor the shareholders shall be held to any personal liability under such order, contract, or obligation." A contract by A. B. as trustee, is the personal undertaking of the trustee, but he may stipulate that he is not to be personally liable except to the extent of the trust estate.

The *shareholders* would probably not be personally liable even in the absence of stipulation if the trustee is not under their control. If the real control is in the shareholders rather than in the trustees, they are liable as partners. Great pains are usually taken to use every precaution so that neither the trustees nor the shareholders, present or future, shall be personally liable by reason of any transaction in connection with the trust property. [Note:—On personal liability see, Williams v. Milton, 215 Mass. 1, 102 N. E. 355, 27 Yale Law Journal, 677; Elliott v. Freeman, 220 U. S. 178; Dana v. Treasurer (Mass. 1917), 116 N. E. 941, 12 Illinois Law Review, 482; Rhode Island Hospital Co. v. Copeland, 39 R. I. 193, 98 Atl. 273; 2 Minn. Law Rev. 401, 13 Mich. Law Rev. 230. (Dec., 1914.).]

Shares.—The interest of the beneficiaries will be represented by shares issued by the trustees. The shares may be of a given par value, such as $100 each, and may be divided into preferred and common shares. It is usually provided that the shares shall be transferrable only on the books of the trustees upon the surrender of the certificate therefor, duly endorsed.

The *rights of shareholders* are similar to those of a stockholder in a corporation, viz., the right to participate in the profits or dividends declared, in the assets on dissolution, and to vote for directors or trustees. So in a trust it is provided that the ownership of shares shall give the shareholders no interest in the property, or right to call for a partition, or for an accounting; no shareholder shall have any other or further rights than those of a shareholder in a corporation. The death of a shareholder or the transfer of his interest, shall not operate to terminate the trust. The only powers over the business which the shareholder reserves, are to consent to alterations or amendments of the trust agreement, or to terminate the trust by a two-thirds vote before the time fixed. Even this degree of control may involve personal liability. (Frost v. Thompson, 219 Mass. 360.) ˙

The trustees are to declare dividends to the shareholders out of the net profits as they may from time to time deem expedient.

Meetings.—The trustees may be authorized to call a meeting of the shareholders at any time, and required to do so upon the written request of the holder or holders of one-fourth of either the preferred or common shares, or the holders of the combined shares. Some action as amendment or the issuance of additional shares may require a two-thirds vote, and other action may be taken by a majority vote of each class of shares present in person or by proxy.

Trustees.—A provision is made for the election and removal of trustees by vote of the shareholders. A succession of trustees can be kept up by means of joint tenancy and provisions in the trust deeds, so that no additional conveyances are necessary to keep up the powers, rights and duties in new trustees.

Upon termination of the trust the trustees are to sell the trust property and divide the proceeds thereof among the shareholders.

Outline of Business Trust Agreement

The following is a summary of a trust agreement with the main points usually provided for:

1. Recital of intended conveyance of property to certain trustees and their successors upon the following trusts. Business name of the trust, "The University Building Trust";

2. Declaration of trust by the trustees; the particular business to be conducted; the trust purposes;

3. Delegation to the trustees of full power and control over the trust property; full power in them and their successors to make it answerable for their acts and contracts; in addition to have all the powers possessed by directors of a corporation;

4. The property of which the trust estate is to consist, (a), property hereby granted; (b), changes of investment; (c), additions;

5. Power of trustees to act singly or by majority; to delegate powers;

6. Power of trustee to stipulate for personal exemption from liability; right of indemnity from the trust funds; right to pledge the trust property for debts and contracts;

7. Exemption of share or certificate holders from assessment or personal liability; all written contracts to contain provisions to this effect;

8. Shares of beneficiaries; certificates, how issued; to give no interest in the property; method of transfer on books; death of shareholder not to affect continuance of trust or to give right to accounting or partition;

9. Division of profits or dividends;

10. Meetings of shareholders; election and removal of trustees;

11. Duration of the trust, which should usually be limited either to certain specified lives of persons mentioned and 21 years; or to a gross period of 21 years;

12. Dissolution or amendment of agreement by vote of two-thirds in value of the certificate holders;

13. Compensation and indemnity of the trustees;

14. Provision for succession of trustees, so that no additional conveyances will be necessary to keep up the title, powers, rights, and duties of the trustees;

15. Authority to the trustees to acquire, hold and dispose of shares in the same manner as if they were not trustees;

16. Authority of trustees to appoint officers and agents and fix their compensation.[1]

---

[1]For forms of trust agreements used in real estate trust and other business trusts, see Wrightington, Unincorporated Assns. Appendix of Forms. Sears, Trust Estates as Business Companies, Appendix. Thompson, Business Trusts.

CHAPTER XIII

PREPARATION AND EXECUTION OF WILLS

Why Make a Will?—The question is frequently asked, why should a man make a will? There are various reasons which may make a will of the utmost importance. The statutes of descent and distribution may not make a satisfactory division of the inheritance. A man having no children may want his wife to get all the property he leaves, and it will probably be necessary to make a will to have his wishes carried out; otherwise part of the property may go to his parents, brothers or sisters. A man having a wife and minor children will probably desire to have the title to his real estate vested in his widow in order that she may more readily deal with the property than she could if minor children have an undivided share in it. To dispose of all your property and to make final provision for your family and dependents is one of the most important and responsible acts of your life.

Every man or woman having property should consider the question what disposition is to be made of this property in event of death and how matters would be managed if the event should happen tomorrow or next week. The failure to make a will means administration according to the Statutes of Descent and Distribution, the provisions of which may be found by reference to the compiled statutes of any particular state.

Any one inclined to omit making a will and to leave his estate to be distributed by an administrator according to statute, should consider the following points:

179

1. That the state laws of descent and distribution were not framed to suit his particular needs and may be unsatisfactory;

2. The uncertainty of the title of the heirs as a matter of record, there being nothing to indicate what particular persons are the heirs;

3. The necessity of partition between several heirs who take by descent as co-tenants;

4. The rights of surviving husband or wife as to curtesy or dower, and the difficulty of assigning it;

5. The relative wealth and conduct of the children or other heirs apparent;

6. The need of creating trusts and prescribing safe policies as to investment for widow or children;

7. The demands of charity and public spirit;

8. The selection of an executor to administer the estate.

The advantages of making a will may be enumerated as in general covering these points:

1. A will establishes, as a matter of record, the particular persons who succeed to the title;

2. Devisees may be given specific parts of the property as absolute owners, while heirs take undivided shares as tenants in common, and partition proceedings may be necessary;

3. An able executor may be selected, preferably an attorney or trust company. Power may be given to the executor to sell property or make mortgages without order of court;

4. A will may avoid trouble in setting off dower. Dower is ordinarily not an adequate provision for the widow;

5. Some heirs apparent, owing to their conduct or wealth, should not participate on the same basis as

others whose need is greater. Some of them may have received advancements in the way of gifts or loans in the lifetime of the testator;

6. Spendthrift trusts may be established which will protect an improvident heir by providing that the capital and income shall not be alienable by him or subject to be taken by his creditors and shall not pass by operation of law. A direct gift might be soon squandered;

7. Employees, servants, charities, and friends may be given legacies;

8. Bonds of executors may be dispensed with to save expense.

Planning a Will.—The planning of any but the simplest will calls for good legal talent and no layman should attempt to draw his own will or that of another. A complicated will which creates trusts, life estates, and limited interests present and future, calls for special legal skill and it may be well to submit a proposed will to two or more lawyers, so that all possible controversy may be avoided. Undue economy in the preparation of wills and reliance upon notaries, justices of the peace, bankers, and other amateur conveyancers frequently results in confusion and litigation.

One who is to act as a draftsman in preparing wills should be prepared with some knowledge of the usual schemes of disposition which experience has approved. He will then be able to advise the testator as to the comparative advantage of the several possible modes of disposition under the particular circumstances of family and property. (For suggestions for preparing wills, see Hayes and Jarman, Concise Forms of Wills; Remsen, Preparation of Wills; Tucker, Forms of Wills; Alexander on Wills, Vol. III., p. 2661.)

The draftsman should get a clear understanding of

the testator's wishes and full information as to his family and estate. The Bankers' Trust Co., of 16 Wall Street, New York City, has prepared a convenient folder entitled, "First Step in Making Your Will," with a set of printed questions designed to draw from the testator his wishes as to the disposition of his property, the kind of gifts to the various donees, and directions as to the method of administering his estate. Suitable blanks are left for memoranda to be furnished the draftsman which will assist him in drawing the will and indicate the donees and the subject-matter. A similar list of questions might well be submitted to the testator to be answered at his leisure.

It is unwise to attempt to settle the terms of any but the simplest wills at a single interview. The lawyer should, if possible, have a preliminary interview in which the situation of the testator's family and his wishes are discussed. At a second interview, for which the lawyer has prepared very careful notes, the possible plans will be discussed in detail. It is usually time enough to submit a draft of the will after this second interview.

Possible Beneficiaries.—The first step in making a will is to consider all the testator's family, dependents and possible beneficiaries, in order to plan the will wisely for the fair distribution of the estate. The claims of husband or wife, children, adopted children, after-born children, illegitimate children, grandchildren, parents, brothers and sisters and their children, other heirs and next of kin, servants, employees, benefactors and friends, educational, religious and charitable institutions should be remembered. The draftsman should see that the names of the legatees are absolutely correct, especially the names of unincorporated societies and institutions. The full names and addresses of the beneficiaries with relationship should be given if possible. The various contingencies of the future as to the persons and property involved must be anticipated, such as the birth and death of children, and other beneficiaries, and the increase or decrease in value of the property. Where all the intended beneficiaries are adults and are to take absolute shares the will may be very simple in form; the whole may be given to the children in equal or unequal shares, subject to a life estate or some proportionate share for the widow, e. g., if there are four adult children, one-sixth to each of the children and two-sixths to the widow.

In Colorado and some western states a married man or woman cannot by will devise or bequeath away from the other spouse more than one-half of his or her property without the consent in writing of such other executed after the death of the testator. In most states the widows' dower is a life estate in one-third of the real property which her husband owned during marriage.

Items of Property.—In distributing the property the draftsman should give attention to the different kinds of property to be distributed, such as the homestead, the testator's business, insurance policies payable to the estate, mortgaged property, securities, household effects, and articles of personal use. The quantity of estate given, the character of the gifts and the description of the property should be put beyond dispute.

The aim should be to give such precise directions regarding the disposition of personal effects, such as works of art, jewelry and silverware, library, clothing, etc., which are to be distributed in specie as to avoid any danger of family quarrels or ill feeling over the division of them.

The gift of a share of the estate, as one-fourth, does not depend on the existence of any specific item of property, whereas a specific gift, as of "my watch," will fail if the gift has been sold or cannot be found. Legacies may be made payable in cash or part in cash and part in such securities as may be held by the estate. Market conditions may be unfavorable and securities may have to be sold at a sacrifice unless distribution in kind is authorized.

Introductory Portions.—The will should commence with a declaration that "This is the last will of ....," giving his name and residence. It should declare that by it the testator means to dispose of all his property at the time of his death, and to exercise all powers of appointment. It should declare that all former wills and codicils are revoked.

The appointment of executors and trustees may conveniently be inserted either at the commencement or at the end of the will. A prudent selection of trustees and executors is of the greatest importance. Care should be taken not to select persons whose duties and whose interests may conflict. It is advisable to select either a lawyer or a trust company to act, rather than a relative interested in the estate, who will have to leave it mostly to some attorney in any case.

Guardians of the person and of the estate of children may be appointed in the will, but this is not to be recommended. The creation of a trust of property for minor children involves less court formalities than a guardianship and is more efficient.

A direction to pay debts and funeral expenses is superfluous unless the testator desires to impose a specific charge upon his real estate, or upon particular chattels.

Provision for Abatement.—Personal estate is, unless otherwise directed, primarily liable for debts and expenses. If there are not sufficient funds to pay all the debts and legacies, abatement or reduction of legacies will result. Those to whom personal property or legacies are given may get little or nothing, while those to whom land is given may get the land free and clear, although the testator would prefer that the land should contribute pro rata, so that each beneficiary would get a proportionate amount, whether his gift was real or personal property. The testator may fix the order of abatement and designate who shall bear the reduction. He should make clear if debts are charged upon land, whether the land is the primary fund, or is merely to supply the deficiency of personal property. He may provide for the exoneration from debts of such gifts as he may wish to prefer. The payment of legacies may be charged upon specific personalty or upon the estate generally, or upon specified realty, or upon realty generally.

General Scheme.—It has been suggested that in framing wills the following plan may well be followed, in order that the disposition may be arranged in some methodical order. [See, I. Hayes, Introduction to Conveyancing (5th Ed.) pp. 412, 434.] Dispose first of the real estate, then of the personalty. Begin with specific devises of real property, placing the more simple, such as immediate devises in fee, before the more complex, such as devises for life with remainder over. In disposing of the personal property, commence with specific bequests of particular chattels or securities, and then proceed to general pecuniary legacies of so much money. The final residuary devise and bequest may dispose of all property not effectively disposed of in the preceding clause. The major portion of the property, real and personal, is sometimes left to be dealt with in the residuary clause. A will should for the most part be made up of general gifts of shares in the estate rather than of gifts of definite legacies or specific items of property. In this way depreciation and shrinkage of property will adjust itself ratably and so of increase.

If the testator has a wife but no children and a large estate he may desire to limit the share of the widow to a life interest and select those who will take the property after her death. In the case of gifts to children the payment or delivery of the gift may be postponed until the age of twenty-five or thirty, an age when a young man is more apt to handle the property wisely than at the bare end of minority. Wills are extremely varied; they range from the simplest of dispositions to the most complicated settlements and trusts. The simplest kind of a will, and one of the commonest, is that by which a man gives the whole of his property to his wife, or the wife gives the whole to her husband, appointing the beneficiary executor.

Where the testator expects to leave both widow and children and a fairly large estate, a common scheme of disposition is to leave the bulk of the real and personal estate to trustees upon trust to sell and convert into cash, to pay a legacy to the wife, and to invest the residue. The wife will be given the income for life and after her death the capital will be divided equally between the children, the issue of a deceased child to take the parent's share.

[The general scheme of the will of a typical testator, providing for wife and children, has been carefully worked out by English conveyancers. It is well explained by Professor A. M. Kales in American Law and Procedure, Vol. V., p. 141, sec. 6 on Drafting a Will. See also, Hayes and Jarman, Concise Forms of Wills (13th Ed.), p. 123. The following paragraphs have been drawn largely from the suggestions given by Professor Kales and by Hayes and Jarman. See also, Elphinstone,

Introduction to Conveyancing, Chap. 12, p. 562 (7th Ed.).]

Frequently all the household effects will be given outright to the widow. It will not be necessary to put into the will an inventory of all the household effects which are to go to the widow; words of general description should be employed. The articles may be described as being all the household furniture and other effects which shall be in or around my house at Chicago, Ill., except money, notes, bonds, stocks, and securities. This clause may further provide, "This bequest shall comprise all my effects, though not strictly household, which are applicable to personal or domestic use, and are not otherwise specifically bequeathed." It is usual to make the gift of these household effects an absolute one, rather than in trust or merely for a life estate.

The bulk of the property other than the household effects and some bequests to various friends, may be devised to trustees for the widow and children. The income from the trust estate may be made payable to the widow for life. She may also be given a pecuniary legacy in priority to all other gifts.

In creating a trust broad powers should be given to the trustees to enable them to administer the estate. There will usually be power to sell, to lease, to mortgage, and to change investments. Directions will be given as to what classes of investments may be made. Power to apportion the trust estate among the beneficiaries and to allow the widow to reside in the testator's house during the time she is entitled to the income of the trust estate, free of rent, may also be given. Elaborate provisions may be needed to give executors and trustees adequate powers of management.

Provision for Children.—While the children are

minors or dependent, it is, of course, expected that the widow will support them out of her income. This may be left to parental affection, or the widow's income and life interest in the whole property may be subject to a charge in favor of the children, as follows:

The income of the trust shall be paid to my wife for her life, she maintaining, educating and bringing up my sons and daughters until they are twenty-one years of age; and if she shall fail to do so to the satisfaction of my trustees, I authorize them in their discretion to retain and appropriate for that purpose so much of the income as they shall think expedient, and pay the residue to my wife for her own support and maintenance.

A power of appointment may be given to the widow to appoint by will to one or more of the children, exclusive of the others, such part or all of the residuary of the estate as she shall see fit. The power should extend to appointing not only to children but to more remote issue, and in such a way as the widow shall deem best. By such a clause the widow retains control over the children. If some are well off, their shares may be reduced. If a son is unreliable, his share may be put under a "spendthrift" trust; but if the widow is partial, or falls under the influence of one of the children, the results may be unjust. It would, therefore, seem advisable to omit the power, unless there is some very strong reason for employing it.

Vested Interest.—Provision for the children may be made in various ways. One method is to make a direct gift to all the children to go to them immediately upon the death or remarriage of the widow. This will give each child a vested interest. Each will acquire an interest at once on the testator's death, subject to the trust for the widow for life. It may be made a postponed vested gift, however, by a clause postponing the termination of the trust and the payment over of each share until the beneficiary reaches a certain age, twenty-one, twenty-five or thirty.

By a clause of *"accruer"* it may be declared that, "in case any of my said children shall die without leaving issue surviving them, the share hereinbefore given to the child so dying (including any further shares accruing under this present clause), shall go and accrue to my other children." This clause of "accruer" is in the nature of a conditional limitation, by which, if a child dies without leaving issue, his share goes to the other brothers and sisters.

Provision should be made for the disposition of income prior to the time of distribution, and income upon vested or expectant shares of each child may be used for his maintenance and education by a general direction to the trustees to apply it for such purposes, or to pay it to parents or guardians, to be applied by them, or to accumulate if not thus spent.

Contingent Gift.—Another plan to provide for the children is by contingent gift, that is, to describe the class who are to take, and to make it contingent upon each member of the class reaching a certain age, say twenty-five, at the time of distribution. This may be provided somewhat as follows:

To such child or children of mine as shall survive me and attain the age of twenty-five, and to the surviving child or children of any child or children of mine who shall be dead at my death, or shall die under the age of twenty-five; provided, that they (such grandchildren) shall take collectively only such share as his or her parent would have taken if such parent had lived to take a vested interest.

While the gift to the children of testator is made contingent on their reaching twenty-five, the gift to the child of any deceased child of the testator is made to it absolutely without waiting for the age of twenty-five; otherwise, there might be a violation of the rule against perpetuities, as it might take effect more than twenty-one years after the death of the widow and all the testator's children.

In the contingent gift, as in the vested one, provision should be made for the disposition of the income prior to the time of distribution; viz., between the termination of the widow's interest and the attainment of the prescribed age.

If all the children are adult and are to take absolute shares, there may be no need of any trust. The widow may be given a life interest and the whole of the property may be given to the children in equal or unequal shares, subject to her life interest, with possibly a trust for partition.

In the case of daughters it may be wise to place their interest beyond the control of present or future husbands by means of a trust for their separate use for life, free from the control of any husband. It may be provided that the daughter's share shall be held after her decease in trust for her children, or more remote descendants, with power of appointment by her will of a life estate to her surviving husband.

It may be desired to charge the beneficiaries with advancements and to equalize the distribution among the children where some have received gifts or loans in the testator's lifetime.

Miscellaneous Suggestions.—Indicate whether the provision for the wife is intended to be in lieu of dower, homestead and widow's award. It is important that the widow be given somewhat more under the will than she would be entitled to without it, as otherwise she will be apt to renounce the will and take independently of it.

Joint ownership and ownership in common by several persons is inconvenient and usually results in partition, which is often an expensive proceeding. A trust for sale and conversion, with discretion in the trustees to suspend indefinitely the exercise of the power of sale, may be advisable and will not prevent the beneficiaries from electing to retain the property as land, or from selling their interests if they wish to do so.

Where movables are to be divided among several legatees, the division may be left to the discretion of the executor.

In a gift to a class of persons, as to the children of X, the period at which the class is to be ascertained should be made clear beyond possibility of doubt.

Where real estate is specifically devised, it is well to examine the title deeds or an abstract of title to avoid misdescription. Courts have no power to correct mistakes in wills.

If the testator devises land which is subject to a mortgage, in most jurisdictions the lien is to be discharged out of the personal estate, unless he otherwise directs by his will. He may direct, either the exoneration of the land, or that the mortgage is not to be paid out of the personalty, and that no recourse is to be had to other realty.

Policies of insurance should be examined by the attorney before the will is executed, and taken into account in the distribution of the property. Proceeds of policies payable to the estate will pass under the residuary clause if not otherwise given.

Children to whom no gift is to be made should be mentioned or should be given a nominal legacy to show that the omission is intentional. It may be provided that after-born children shall share equally with children who are named.

The lapse of gifts should be provided for. If a

person to whom a gift is made be no longer living at the death of the testator, the gift will fail even if made to the donee and his heirs. The will may direct that the gift shall pass to the children or descendants of the donee in case he be not living at the testator's death. Statutes often protect the descendants of children and grandchildren in this respect, but a devise of real estate to a stranger, or to the testator's father or mother or brother or sister, or other relative, not a child of grandchild, will usually fail or lapse unless provision is made. Many wills are defective in not providing what shall be done with a gift, in event of the death of the donee before the testator. Do not rely on the residuary clause for this purpose.

A provision may be employed to prevent contest of the will that "if any heir or devisee contests this will, he shall receive no part of my estate." It would be advisable to make a gift over stating who shall take his share in case of breach of the condition. [See note Re Hite, 21 L. R. A. (N. S.) 953.]

An existing paper, such as a letter or schedule of property, may be incorporated in a will by reference to it, but this must be sufficiently clear and definite to identify the paper distinctly. Moreover, the document must be actually in existence, and referred to as existing at the time the will is executed. A person cannot reserve power for future testamentary directions, without the statutory formalities.

Avoid the rule in Shelley's Case. Do not give property ·to A for life and after the death of A, then to his heirs," or "the heirs of his body." The effect is a gift to A but not to the heirs. Avoid in all cases, so far as possible, making a gift to a person's heirs, or the heirs of his body.

The terms "heirs" and "heirs of the body" are

erms which must be used with great caution, especially if they are intended as words of purchase, hat is, as description of the donees, rather than of imitation, indicating the estate given their ancestor. (Black v. Jones, 264 Ill. 548.)

The phrase "die without issue" is ambiguous; it should be indicated whether "without having had issue," or, "without issue or descendants living at his death," is intended.

Avoid offending the rule against perpetuities. No future interest subject to a condition precedent is good, unless the condition must be fulfilled within 21 years after some life or lives in being and 21 years; or, if no life is specified, then within a period of 21 years. A devise to all of the testator's grandchildren, when they shall arrive at 30 years of age, would be void. Provide as to what shall be the effect on the other gifts, if any clause of the will is held void under the rule against perpetuities.

The terms *"per stirpes"* and *"per capita"* are frequently used to define the proportions in which several beneficiaries are to take. If the donees take *per capita,* they take equal shares. If the donees take *per stirpes,* they take by right of representation the share which their parent would have taken. Thus if X dies, leaving two children, A and B, each takes half. If B dies first, leaving two children, C and D, then A takes one-half and C and D take one-fourth each. If several beneficiaries who stand in different relationships to the testator are to share a gift, it is well to state with special clearness the proportion which each is to take.

A spendthrift trust may be created in many jurisdictions by which trustees will hold the property and pay the income to the beneficiary, but not subject to

any claim of his creditors or to any power of alienation by him. If a son is dissipated or incompetent to
manage his property, or if a daughter has an untrust-
worthy husband, it may be prudent to create such a
trust, putting both principal and income beyond danger of being lost or wasted by the beneficiary.

It may be advisable to give the executors powers
for the continuance of the individual or partnership
business of the testator, but great care must be taken
as to such a provision.

Avoid precatory words of recommendation in creating a trust and impose a definite obligation on the
trustee.

It is often convenient to authorize the payment of
legacies which may be small to the parents or guardians of infant legatees, with a direction that the receipts of those persons shall discharge the executors or
trustees.

In leaving property to "children" as a class, it
should be ascertained that all the children intended to
be benefited are legitimate. If any of them are illegitimate, they should be mentioned by name.

The names of charitable corporations and societies
should be carefully ascertained, as mistakes are often
made causing litigation as to which one is intended.

Inheritance taxes must be considered by a testator
and his attorney in planning the disposition of his
property. Instead of giving all the property to the
children, the testator may be well advised to make
substantial gifts also to his grandchildren, or to his
son's wife. Bequests to such persons may reduce the
amount of tax against his estate, as each beneficiary
may be entitled to an exemption and may take the
property at the lowest rate.

It may be well to leave vested rather than contin-

gent remainders wherever possible. A contingent devise under the Illinois and New York Statutes imposes
the tax on the assumption that the contingency will
happen which will give the highest possible tax. Take
the case of a testator who wishes to give his wife a
life estate, the property then to go to his children.
If he makes a devise to his wife for life, then to such
of his issue as are living at the time of her death, and
if none of them are living, then to such of my next of
kin as are then living; this means no exemption, and
possibly a high rate of tax. If on the other hand he
leaves his property to his wife for life, with remainder
equally to A, B, and C, (naming his children), in fee,
A, B, and C will take vested remainders and an exemption of $20,000 will be allowed for each child under
the Illinois statutes. (Cecil Barnes, Drafting of Wills
and Inheritance Taxes, 12 Illinois Law Review, 636.)

It may be well to provide for the payment of inheritance taxes out of the estate as a whole, that is
out of the residuary estate, in order to relieve the
various legatees and devisees.

The estates given to devisees must be defined with
special care. It is often difficult to determine whether
the devisee was to take for life or in fee, and whether a
vested or a contingent interest. To give a life interest in
personal property is not usually convenient or advisable,
unless by way of trust.

A condition in general restraint of marriage is invalid. A condition that the devisee shall not alienate
is void. So if a testator devises real and personal estate to A and his heirs, but in case of his death without disposing of it by deed or will then to B, A takes
absolute title and the gift over to B is void. But if
the will gives A a life estate only, with an absolute
power of disposition by deed or will, a gift over to

B may be made to take effect if A does not exercise his power.

A gift may be made to A for life, with power to consume, followed by a gift over to B of "what remains" at A's death, if any. A better way to accomplish the purpose is by a trust, that is a gift to the trustees to manage the property, collect the income, and pay the income, and if needed part of the principal, to A for life and on his death to deliver what remains to B. This affords more protection to B and is less likely to lead to dispute.

The testator may make provision in his will for the purchase of a burial lot in a cemetery and the erection of a monument and the care of it. It may be wise, however, to leave this to the voluntary choice of the family and to make any suggestions on the subject by separate letter. Direction as to the disposition of the body by burial or cremation and as to the funeral should be given in a letter to be opened immediately after death rather than in the will, as the will is frequently not read until after the burial.

There is no better monument to a man's memory than a well-considered gift to some charitable purpose. It is very unwise to confine too closely the charitable purposes, but the institution or trustees should be given a wide discretion to use the income and even the principal as it is most needed under changing conditions.

Formalities of Execution.—Great care must be exercised to comply with all the formalities of execution and attestation required by the statutes governing the validity of the will. If one changes his domicile from one state to another he should see that his will complies with the law of the state where he now resides, and if it affects land he should see that it complies wth the law of the state where the land is situated.

It is usually required that a will be signed *at the end* by the testator himself, or by some other person in his presence and by his direction. It must be attested in the presence of the testator by two or more competent witnesses who saw the testator sign the will or acknowledge the signature in their presence. It is regarded as a wise precaution that in the case of type-written wills the testator should sign every sheet to prevent substitutions. It is well to have at least three witnesses who are friends or acquaintances of the testator and younger than he; their addresses should be given. It is important to avoid infants, incompetents, heirs at law, legatees or devisees, or husband or wife of a legatee, or of an executor, as witnesses. Gifts to a subscribing witness or to the wives or husbands of subscribing witnesses are usually declared void. The witnesses should watch the testator sign the will or see him acknowledge the signature as his, if already made, and should themselves sign as witnesses in the presence of the testator and at his request after he has signed the will. The witnesses should also sign as such in the presence of each other and all should remain together until the will is fully executed. It is not necessary that the terms of the will be read or shown to the witnesses, as they merely attest the signature. "Publication" of the will consists of a declaration by the testator that the instrument is his last will and testament.

The following is a *form of attestation clause* which embodies the requirements of the statutes of most states:

The above instrument, consisting of .... typewritten (or written) pages, each bearing on its margin the signature of the above named .... was by said .... signed, sealed, declared and published to be his (or her) last will and testament, in our presence. At his (or her) request and in his (or her) presence and in the presence of each other, believing him (or her) to be of sound and disposing mind and memory, we have hereunto set our hands as witnesses.

.... Residence ....
.... Residence ....

Suggestions on Execution.—The testator should tell the witnesses that this is his will and his signature, and that he wants them to witness it. The statute usually calls for two attesting witnesses, but it is well to have three or four. It often happens that the witnesses to a will are dead, or have moved away so that they cannot be found, and that no one can be produced who can identify their handwriting. The witness should write, in addition to his signature, his place of residence. In New York and some states his failure to do so may subject him to a penalty.

The signatures of the witnesses would be sufficient without an attestation clause. It is not required by statute, and the fact that it is omitted would not affect the validity of the will. It is very useful, however, as a method of calling attention to the observance of the required formalities. Sometimes when the witnesses are dead or cannot be produced, it may be of great value as presumptive evidence of due execution and capacity.

All alterations, interlineations and erasures should be initialed and reference to them should be made in the attestation clause.   No alterations should be made after execution.

A *codicil* is a supplement to a former will made by the testator, to be taken as part of it, making some addition to or change in the former disposition.   It requires the same formalities as the execution of a new will.

Custody of Will.—It is quite customary for a client to assume that he will keep his will in his own safe deposit box.   This is a common practice, but it is an inconvenient place for a man to keep his will.   It probably means that the next of kin will have to get an order of court to open the safe deposit box to get the will, and this may cause delay and annoyance. The best place for a will is ordinarily either in the hands of the executor nominated in the will, or in the hands of the lawyer whom the testator would wish to have charge of the administration of his estate, who is usually the lawyer who draws the will.   In any case, the attorney who draws the will should keep an exact copy, as a correct copy may usually be admitted to probate in case of loss of the original.   A will may be executed in duplicate to avoid loss.

Statement of Assets.—It will be advisable for the testator to file from time to time with his will, or in his safe deposit box, an inventory or statement of his assets and liabilities and the location of his property, particularly when he does not keep complete books of account.   It is often difficult to locate bank accounts and safe deposit boxes, to find securities, and to ascertain the condition of the estate.

Simple Form of Will to Wife

I, John Smith, of Chicago, Illinois, do hereby make, publish and declare this my last Will and Testament, in manner and form following:

First. I revoke all former wills and codicils.

Second. I devise and bequeath all my estate, real and personal, wherever situate, to my wife, Mary Smith, to have and to hold, absolutely and forever.

Third. I nominate and appoint my said wife and the .... Trust Company of the City of Chicago, to be executrix and executor, without bond, of this, my last Will and Testament.

In Witness Whereof, I have hereunto subscribed my name and affixed my seal, this 1st day of August, 19...., in the presence of John Doe and Richard Roe, whom I have requested to become attesting witnesses hereto.

(Signature of testator)
John Smith   (Seal)

(Attestation clause: see form above.)

Skeleton Form of Will

I, ..., of the city of ...., county of .... and state of ....,
being of sound mind and memory and of the age of ...... years, do make, publish and declare this to be my last will and testament, hereby revoking all other wills and codicils by me heretofore executed:

First. I direct that all my just debts and funeral expenses be paid.

Second. I give and bequeath to, etc. (Personalty).

Third. I give and devise to, etc. (Realty).

Fourth. I give, devise and bequeath to, etc., (the rest, residue and remainder of my property, real and personal.)

Fifth. I hereby nominate and appoint ...., of ...., to be the executor of this, my last will and testament (and direct that he be not required to give security for the performance of his duties as such executor).

In witness whereof, I have hereunto set my hand and seal this ...... day of ...., A. D. 19....

.........................(Seal)

The above instrument consisting of ...... pages and lines, was on the day of the date thereof declared and acknowledged to us by ...., the testator therein mentioned to be his last will and testament, and we were present and saw the said .... sign and seal the same, and we, at his request and in his actual presence, and in the presence of each other, do sign our names as attesting witnesses to said will and we verily believe the said ....to be of sound mind and memory.
.....................(Seal)   Residing at ....
.....................(Seal)   Residing at ....

CODICIL

Codicil to the last will and testament of me,...... .... which bears date on the .... day of .... A. D. 1910........

Whereas by said will I have provided .... in lieu place and stead of said provision, which I now revoke and annul I now provide as follows, that is to say, I give, etc.

And in all other respects I do confirm my said will.

In witness whereof, I have hereunto set my hand and seal this .... day of .... A. D. 19.......

.....................(Seal)

The above instrument was at the date thereof declared to us by the said ...., the testator therein mentioned, to be a codicil to his last will and testament dated ...., and we were present and saw him sign said codicil, and he at the same time acknowledged to us that he had signed and sealed the same as a codicil to his said last will and testament, and we therefore at his request and in his presence and in the presence of each other have signed and do sign our names as attesting witnesses to the same, believing the said .... to be of sound mind and memory.

.....................(Seal)   Residing at ....
.....................(Seal)   Residing at ....

(Compare this attesting clause with that to form for the will.)

Requisition for Will—No. 1
(University of Wisconsin Law School)

Dear Sir:

I am going abroad for an extended journey, and before I go I want to make my will. As you know I have a wife and three children and I have farms in the Dakotas and Minnesota, and a business block in Illinois, beside some timber land in Michigan. But most of my property is in mortgages, stocks and bonds. I want to give my wife the homestead and all its furnishings including pictures and books. I also want to give her two thousand dollars in cash and my business block in °Illinois. I want to give my son, John, my Dakota farms; to Henry, my Minnesota and Michigan lands, and to my daughter, Mary, $10,000 cash.

Then the rest of my estate I want to put in trust in some trust company that you can recommend, they to take the income and pay one-quarter of it annually to my wife so long as she lives and one-quarter to each of the children until they reach the age of 35 respectively, when each one is to get his share.

The one-quarter on which my widow is to get the interest during life to be added on her death to the three-quarters of which my children have the use and be disposed of finally in the same way.

I want my wife to be executrix without any bond. You know the descriptions of my properties. Please have this all ready for me by Wednesday, April 8th, when I will call for it.

Yours truly,

Henry James.

Prepare the will complete, including all necessary signatures and attestation clauses, typewritten if possible—but otherwise with special attention to clearness and legibility—in fact, prepare the will exactly as though it were the completed will of an actual client.

REQUISITION FOR WILL—No. 2
O. L. McCaskill—Methods of Teaching Practice
(II. Cornell Law Quarterly, p. 304)

Henry Jones desires you to draft his will. He is a man of considerable wealth, consisting of various kinds of real and personal property. He is interested as a stockholder and director in several large businesses, in some of which he has a controlling interest. He and William Jenks are partners in the lumber and coal business under the name of Jones-Jenks Lumber & Coal Company. He has several life insurance policies payable to his estate. He has a wife from whom he has become estranged, although they live in the same house for the sake of their children and appearances. He has two daughters —Jane, 7 years old, and Emily, 19 years old; and a son—George, 22 years old, who is bright, and has many of his father's characteristics, but is wild and extravagant. The son is attending a university, and is devoting most of his attention to athletics and girls. Emily has shown a liking for a young man whom Jones thinks is courting her for her money. He desires to keep his estate intact as nearly as possible five years after his death, and at that time to give George and Emily each a fourth of his estate, provided George has settled down, and shown some aptitude for business, and provided Emily has not married a money-seeker. In the event of either of these contingencies not happening, he desires that each be paid the income only from his or her fourth, and that the principal be adequately protected until the contingencies happen. He desires Jane to get one-fourth when she attains her majority, subject to the same provisions as are made for Emily. He desires his wife to have the income from one-fourth for life, and this discontinued if she re-marries. On death or re-marriage of his wife he desires her portion to be equally distributed among the children. If a child dies before the time of distribution, his or her share shall be distributed among the survivors, unless there are grandchildren, when they are to take. If his beneficiaries should all die before him, or after him without heirs, his desire is that some charitable disposition be made of his property, either to further investigation into a cure for cancer, or to found a hospital for tuberculosis patients.

Draft the will, providing for all possible contingencies, including death of several in a common disaster. If the will of testator cannot be accomplished in any particular, accomplish it as nearly as possible, and attach a note of explanation. Have will properly executed, and attach the best attestation clause you can devise. If you do not have sufficient particulars in any respect, fill in as you would recommend or suggest to testator.

REQUISITION FOR WILL—No. 3

Prepare a will for Adam Bede, to carry out the following general instructions, including all necessary signatures and an attestation clause. The testator leaves a wife, Eve, and three children, Cain, Abel and Sarah. He has farms in various states, but most of his property is in mortgages, stocks and bonds.

1. Provide for three specific legacies to testator's friends or more distant relatives.

2. Give the wife the testator's homestead, household effects, pictures and books, also $2,000 in cash.

3. Give the rest and residue of the estate to some trust company, with ample powers to sell, invest, partition, etc.

4. The income from the trust estate is to be paid to the widow for life, but she is to use at least *one-half* of it for the education and support of the children.

5. Give the widow a power of appointment by will to establish a spendthrift trust for any of the children, specifying the terms of the trust.

6. Provide a gift to each of the children in default of appointment, after the termination of the widow's interest, contingent upon reaching the age of thirty.

7. Provide for the disposition of the income by the trustees prior to the time of distribution or vesting for the education and maintenance of the children or their issue by way of a spendthrift trust.

8. Provide a method of supplying successors to the trustees in cases of vacancy.

9. Appoint an executor with power of sale.

10. Provide for forfeiture of benefits by anyone contesting the will and gift over to another.

11. Provide any other clauses which you may deem necessary to make a complete testamentary scheme of disposition; e. g., as to shares of grandchildren or their issue.

(Hayes & Jarman, Concise Forms of Wills, and Tucker, Testamentary Forms.)

Trust Deed as a Substitute for a Will.—In some exceptional cases a deed of trust rather than a will may be employed to dispose of part or the whole of an estate. The deed or trust may be so drawn as to reserve the use, income, and control of the property during the donor's life, and direct its disposition after his death. The great advantage of this method is that a declaration of trust is a present transaction which becomes effective during the lifetime of the donor, and obviates the delay, executor's fees, attorney's fees, and court costs incident to a will with its probate and administration proceedings.

But putting income producing property in trust the widow may be relieved of the care and management of investments. So other beneficiaries who are too young or too old or too inexperienced to manage property wisely for themselves may receive the income from trustees.

By means of a trust an impartial administration of the common fund may be provided for several beneficiaries who may take present and future interests. In this way some may be restricted to a share of the income and the principal preserved for others to be divided at the termination of the trust.

A trustee is usually preferable to a guardian. Property may be given to a trustee for the education and maintenance of a minor without appointing any guardian at all. The trustee should be given full power to sell, mortgage, and lease any and all real estate and change investments, in order that he may have authority to do what is needed to administer the property. The trustee should be authorized to retain as part of the trust property any securities which the donor may own and to invest at his discretion in certain classes of securities. Otherwise he will be restricted in making investments to those very conservative classes authorized by law for trust funds. The income of these "legal investments" is usually much less than others, equally safe, yielding a larger income return.

The trustee should be authorized to treat all stock dividends and extra cash dividends and distribution of "rights" as "income"; to avoid question whether they belong to the principal.

Spendthrift Trust.—A spendthrift trust may be established by providing that "no person entitled to a share of the net income of the trust estate shall have the right to anticipate the same, nor to sell, assign, mortgage, or encumber his share in the trust estate or any part of it, or the income therefrom, and no share in the trust estate shall be liable for his or her debts or be subject to garnishment, execution, attachment, creditor's bill or other legal or equitable process."

A present disposition giving rights to the beneficiary before the death of the maker may avoid inheritance taxes. The power of revocation during the life of the donor may be reserved, as in the case of a will, but this will probably impose an inheritance tax on those taking after his death. The advantage of a will, on the other hand, is that it does not effect or impair the title to the property during the life of the testator and may be drawn to cover all the property which he may have at death. (Remsen on Preparation of Wills, p. 5; Thulin, Formal Creation of a Trust, XI Ill. Law Rev. 619; Tiffany, Forms, p. 1282; Meldahl v. Wallace, 270 Ill. 220; People v. Northern Trust Co., 289 Ill. 479.)

Taxability of trust deeds which reserve power of revocation.—Where a person transfers property to a trustee for the benefit of widow, children, or other persons, reserving to himself a power of revocation, the question frequently arises, whether on the death of the donor this property is taxable as a transfer intended to take effect in possession or enjoyment at death. The presence of a power of revocation in the deed is strong *prima facie* evidence that no absolute transfer takes place until death and that the property is therefore taxable.

The Federal estate tax has substantially the same provision as the New York Transfer Tax, taxing transfers intended to take effect at death. In Regulations of the Treasury Department issued August 8, 1919, Article 25, it is expressly provided that a transfer by way of trust where the grantor reserves a power of revocation is taxable on the grantor's death. If this ruling is sustained by the courts, the estate must also pay a federal tax.

In a recent case in Illinois it was held that property conveyed by a trust deed, in which the donor reserved merely a power of revocation was not taxable on the death of the donor. In case, however, the income for life is reserved to the donor, the transfer would be taxable at his death. [People v. Northern Trust Co. (1919) 289 Ill. 475; 124 N. E. 662; People v. Kelley, 218 Ill. 509; 28 Harvard Law Rev. 334; 29 Yale Law Journal, 464; Bullen v. Wisconsin, 240 U. S. 625.]

In drawing up trust deeds, therefore, it is advisable to omit a power of revocation or other powers reserved to the grantor, unless such powers are deemed actually essential to the protection of the grantor. The choice is between taxability of the property upon the grantor's death, in case such powers are included, and lack of protection of the grantor in case such powers are omitted, for in such a case the trust cannot be revoked without consent of the beneficiaries.

REQUISITION FOR A DECLARATION OF TRUST BY DEED

(See Formal Creation of a Trust *Inter Vivos,* XI. Ill. Law Rev. p. 619, by Frederick Thulin; People v. Northern Trust Co., 289 Ill. 475, 477.)

Prepare a declaration of trust drawn between Robert Lloyd, the creator and founder and the X. Trust Co. of Chicago, Illinois:

1. Introduction, names of parties and date;

2. Recital of purpose;

3. Operative words of conveyance to the trust company. The real property and the securities should be carefully described. The personal property may be transferred to the trustee by indorsing or delivering the securities. The real property may be transferred by a deed to the X. Trust Co. as trustee, separate and apart from the trust instrument. The recording of this instrument will show legal title in the trustee, putting the purchaser on notice, but will keep secret the provisions of the trust;

4. Statement of the object of the trust with the greatest care. The said trustee is to hold and manage the above mentioned real and personal property, collect the income and pay the same to the said Robert Lloyd, during and for his natural life; then to his wife for life; and after her death the property shall be distributed equally among his children, A. B. and C. [or shall be distributed among such of his children and grandchildren as are living at the time of his death.]

5. Shares of deceased children to go to their issue;

6. Clause of accruer (in case of vested interests). If any of the said children shall die without issue surviving said Robert Lloyd before the said Robert Lloyd, the share of such deceased child shall be divided equally among the other shareholders of the trust estate;

7. If all the children of said Robert Lloyd shall die before him, leaving no issue, then the property shall be transferred by the said trustee to the X University;

8. A provision allowing the creator of the trust to modify it, or to revoke it at any time by notice in

writing to the trustee, upon which the trustee is to re-convey to the creator discharged from all trusts;

9. A provision for the appointment of a successor in trust, in case of resignation of trustee;

10. A provision with reference to the right of the trustee to invest trust funds in various securities other than "legal investments";

11. A provision with reference to a right of the trustee to sell personal or real property and to lease real property; care for and protect the same; to collect rents and income therefrom; to pay taxes and assessments; to repair and rebuild buildings if destroyed; to insure; to bring and defend legal proceedings concerning the same; to appoint agents to negotiate and prepare leases, and to assume entire charge of affairs;

12. A provision with reference to the method of apportionment of the property among several beneficiaries when such division becomes necessary by the terms of the trust;

13. A provision with reference to indemnifying the trustee and the matter of trustee's fees and trustee's bond;

14. A provision that all stock dividends, "rights," and extraordinary cash dividends shall be treated as income.

Exercise in Criticism of Freak Trust

Criticise the following deed executed as a substitute for a will, reserving a life estate in favor of grantor and creating contingent remainders in grantor's daughters, *et al.* Meldahl v. Wallace, 270 Ill. 220:

On February 6, 1911, Eline E. Johnson made acknowledged and delivered to her three daughters Clara Amalia Meldahl, Olga Therese Wallace and

Alice Eline T. West, the following deed, which was accepted by the grantees in writing, under their hands and seals, as part of the deed.

This indenture witnesseth, that I, the grantor, Eline T. Johnson, of the city of Chicago, in the county of Cook and State of Illinois, for and in consideration of the sum of one dollar to me in hand paid, and other good, valuable and sufficient consideration, the receipt of all which is hereby acknowledged, do hereby convey and warrant to my daughters, Clara Amalia Meldahl and Olga Therese Wallace, of the city of Chicago, and Alice Eline T. West, of the city of Los Angeles and State of California, the following described real estate—to wit: (Describing four tracts of real estate). In trust, nevertheless, with the rights, powers and authority and for the uses and purpose hereinafter set forth.

I, the grantor, Eline T. Johnson, do by these presents grant, assign, convey, alien, transfer and set over unto said trustees, and the survivor or survivors of them, all and singular, the stocks, bonds, promissory notes, debts, choses in action, evidences of debt, property and effects of every description, real, personal, and mixed, belonging to me the said grantor, wherever the same may be situated, except my personal goods and chattels and household effects, in trust, nevertheless, with the rights, powers and authority and for the uses and purposes hereinafter set forth.

To have and to hold the title to all my said estate herein conveyed, both realty and personalty, for and during my natural life, and upon my decease to divide the same equally between themselves, and to convey the same when such a division has been agreed upon, and in case of their not being able to agree upon a division, that they, or any one of them, may apply to a court of competent jurisdiction to appoint a commissioner or commissioners to effect an equitable and equal division of the same. I hereby give my said daughters, and each of them, the power to will or devise their respective share or interest herein, both as to realty and personalty, as they see fit, and that in case of the decease of any of my daughters herein named, intestate, before my death, then in that case the children of such deceased daughter shall take their parent's share, both as to realty and personalty, and if any such deceased daughter so dying intestate leaves a husband surviving, that the husband have the same right to the use and enjoyment of both the realty and personalty and the benefit of it as given by the statutes of the State of Illinois. Said trustees, and the survivor or survivors of them to have the joint custody of all my personalty, hereby conveyed, transferred and set over to them, jointly with myself, it being hereby agreed that no transfer or conveyance shall be made of the same, or any part thereof, without the concurrence of myself and any two of my said trustees.

And I, the grantor, Eline T. Johnson, do herein and hereby reserve unto myself the right to manage and control the real estate as to the renting, repairing and collecting of rents and appointing agents to rent or collect the same, and also reserve to myself the full, free and unreserved control and use of all the income of my said estate, both real, personal and mixed, during my natural life, intending that all the rents of my real estate shall be paid promptly to me or any agent that I may designate, and that all the income or interest of any evidences of indebtedness or dividends of any stock that I may hold shall be paid directly to me as the same may become due and payable, without having to go through the hands of my said trustees.

The conveyance made herein to said trustees shall be to said trustees and the survivor or survivors of them, and all the rights, powers and authority herein given said trustees shall be to them and the survivor or survivors of them.

Witness my hand and seal this fourth day of February, A. D. 1911.

Eline T. Johnson   (Seal)

We, the undersigned, named in the foregoing instrument as trustees thereunder, do hereby accept the trust in said instrument confided to us.

Witness our hand and seal this sixth day of February, A. D. 1911.

Clara Amalia Meldahl   (Seal)
Olga Therese Wallace   (Seal)
Alice Eline T. West   (Seal)

By Clara Amalia Meldahl, her attorney in fact.

CHAPTER XIV

EXAMINATION OF ABSTRACTS OF TITLE

Importance of Examination.—Under our present recording system no conveyance may prudently be accepted without laborious examination of the title. Purchasers or lenders entering into contracts for the purchase or mortgage of real estate should always insist upon the examination of the title, before they part with the money in their grasp for a mere piece of paper, which purports to give them houses or lands.

Opinions of Counsel.—A purchaser of land will ordinarily bring to his lawyer an abstract of title already prepared from the records and files in the county recorder's office, tax collector's office, court files or other offices, and request his opinion upon the title whose successive steps it displays. An American abstract is a condensed history of the title to land, consisting of a summary of all the deeds, mortgages and proceedings of record, which in any manner affect the title, showing the origin and the whole course of devolution of the title, without resort to the registry of deeds and other legal depositories. The abstract is turned over to counsel, who critically examines each instrument shown; notes any breaks or irregularities in the chain of conveyances, and reports his opinion as to the person in whom the title is vested, and the defects in the title, such as failure of the wife of a grantor to join in some deed, defective acknowledgments, taxes a lien, undivided interest outstanding in heir, or irregularities in probate sales. If one link in the title is a judicial sale, or a sale by an executor, administrator or guardian, a sheriff's sale on execution or a tax title, the lawyer must examine every step in the proceedings minutely and critically.

Root of Title.—Title examination is carried back to some undisputed source of title, either to its inception in a patent from the government, or to some well authenticated origin at some time in the past sufficiently remote to bar all adverse claims. In England this period was sixty years until fixed at forty by statute. In many Western states a patent from the government or public grant to individuals is recognized as the foundation of title, and the devolution is often traced from that to the date of examination. The statutory period of limitation is too short to afford protection to the purchaser; title must be shown beyond the period of any doubt, including the removal of any personal disabilities of adverse claimants, such as infancy or absence from the state.

Infirmities of Record Title.—An apparently perfect chain of title may appear on the records, yet by reason of defects outside the records, such as the forgery of some signature, the incompetency of some grantor, this apparently perfect title may be nothing but worthless paper. A record of deeds cannot identify parties or make an empty title good. Title can never be demonstrated as an established fact from records; it may only be presented as an inference more or less reliable so far as the documentary transfers show. Adverse possession may have extinguished it. One buys lands subject to the rights of the possessor, whatever they may be, as by contract or unrecorded deed, and subject to easements, such as rights of way acquired by adverse user or prescription or impled grant. Records afford protection against previous unrecorded deeds, mortgages, contracts, liens, trusts, etc., but not against adverse possession, prescription, lack of legal title in grantor owing to forged, unauthorized, undelivered or altered deeds, or incompetency of grantors. Such defects appear, if at all, only from inspection of the original documents or from inquiries about the grantors and grantees, their capacity and connection with the land.

Opinions Advising on Title.—The object of examination of title is to determine in whom the abstract shows presumptive evidence of title, and what are the defects and objections to which the title is subject. In writing a letter of opinion on the title, the attorney will usually refer to the abstract by caption and description of the land and give a concise opinion based upon the abstract and the defects which it discloses. He will usually place the title in some individual or person as owner, subject to certain enumerated defects and objections, including any encumbrances or liens, and doubts arising as to the description or as to the construction and legal effect of any instrument. He will be careful to base his opinion on the title as disclosed by the abstract and will say that "from an examination of the abstract, the title to said lands appears to be now vested in John Doe, subject to the following defects and objections." He will leave it to the client to accept or reject the title or cure the defects. In general, he should state briefly his practical conclusions without argument or technical terminology. In case of defects appearing in the abstract he may suggest methods by which these defects may be removed.

The attorney in examining abstracts must have such a knowledge of real property law as to be able to ascertain the effect of the various instruments which are abstracted. These may include all possible methods of transferring or affecting title, and when in doubt the attorney will have to study the statutes and decisions of the state which govern the matter. He has to be constantly on his guard to see that he does not overlook defects in the form of the execution of conveyances, defects in the estate or description of the property, mortgages or liens on the property, inheritance taxes, outstanding rights to dower and curtesy, restrictions on the use and numerous other matters.

The opinion on the title should warn the client that there are various matters and defects which may impair the title, which the abstract and the public records cannot disclose, such as right of parties in possession under unrecorded deeds, leases or contracts, surveys, fence lines, incapacity of grantors to convey, non-delivery and forgery of deeds.

Diagram of Title.—The first thing to do when you are about to examine an abstract is to locate the land by making a diagram, showing the exact piece of property in question. A tabulation of the links in the chain of title may be used to check up possible breaks and clear up complications. A diagram of the title may be made by drawing a horizontal line at the top of the page, and writing above it the name of the owner who is taken as the root of title, often the United States. Each step or transfer of title is shown by drawing a line down from the name of the grantor, or transferor to the name of the grantee or transferee. Where the whole property is transferred absolutely, a perpendicular line is drawn down to a horizontal line, above which the transferee's name is written.

Where the grantor does not convey his whole estate, a horizontal line is carried out to the right or left; in case of an encumbrance, mortgage or lease, to the right; in case of a life estate or a conveyance of a portion of the property, to the left. Then a perpendicular line is drawn to the name of the transferee. This will indicate the branching out and sub-division of the title.

It is convenient to note the date of each transfer at the left of each perpendicular, with a reference to a number in the abstract where it is given. A notation of the estate granted and of the nature of the instrument may be indicated by abbreviation at the right, as W. D. for warranty deed, Q. C. for quit-claim deed. Such a diagram or analysis gives a comprehensive view of the course of title, and thus lessens the risk of overlooking any encumbrance, and helps the examiner to trace the effect of each different transfer.

Patents.—The abstract should begin with some acknowledged source of title, usually a patent from United States government, or from one of the states. In many cases the patent has never been called for or recorded, a receiver's receipt or other preliminary document being the only recorded evidence of title. The full legal title is not conveyed until the patent is issued. It need not be recorded, but recording is the best evidence that a patent was issued. If the patent has been issued, but not recorded, get an exemplified copy and have it recorded. If no patent was ever issued, steps should be taken to procure its issue. The patent often is not issued until after many transactions have occurred, but when issued it relates back to the date of purchase and enures to the heirs, devisees or assigns of the purchaser. [2 Tiffany on Real Property (2nd Ed.) sec. 426.]

Deeds.—All the essential parts of the abstracted transfers have to be considered to judge of their effect upon the title. The most common instruments of transfer are, of course, deeds. In examining a deed the following suggestions will give some idea of what must be looked for:

1. Compare the date of the deed and the date of acknowledgment and the recording. If there is a discrepancy this will put the examiner on inquiry;

2. Compare the names of the persons who are grantors in the deed with the name of the grantee in the preceding deed. Great care must be taken to preserve identity of names, and object if there is any discrepancy in names and initials;

3. Watch for recitals or references to other instruments, like contracts, which may affect the title. Observe the recital of consideration and words of grant;

4. Does the grantor's wife join in the deed, or does the deed recite that the grantor was single?

5. Check the description of the property with the greatest care;

6. Make note of any reservations, exceptions, covenants or conditions affecting the title;

7. Are the words of limitation in the habendum consistent with the granting clause? What is the nature of the estate granted?

8. Scrutinize the signatures and sealing;

9. Acknowledgment and attestation, if required.

Acknowledgment.—The certificate of acknowledgment must be carefully inspected in the light of the statutes of the particular state, regarding the manner of taking acknowledgments. The contents of the certificate of acknowledgment usually are (1) venue, that is the state or county where taken; (2) date of acknowledgment, name, title, and jurisdiction of officer; "Before me a notary public in and for the county of Cook, etc."

(3) Personal appearance of the grantor;

(4) Personally known to the officer;

(5) Acknowledgment of his signature as his free act and deed;

(6) Officer's signature;

(7) In some states officer's seal is essential, and omission of seal is fatal error;

(8) In some states the date when the officer's commission expires, and release of homestead.

A recorded deed or instrument not acknowledged according to the law is in most states not constructive notice to subsequent creditors and purchasers, and one who has a deed or mortgage which he fails properly to record, may have his title cut off by a subsequent deed, mortgage or attachment, duly recorded.

A certificate of magistracy or authority of the notary or justice of the peace may be required where the deed is acknowledged outside the state where the land lies. Acknowledgment before an officer who is interested in the conveyance, is void, e. g., if he is a stockholder of the grantee corporation. Formerly acknowledgments of married women had to be taken after examination separate and apart from the husband to bar dower, and it may be necessary to examine the law in force at the date of the conveyance. To overcome a faulty certificate of acknowledgment, parties must reappear before the notary and acknowledge the execution of the old deed or of a new deed for the same property.

Power of Attorney.—The authority of those executing a deed or mortgage for a corporation should appear. If the deed or conveyance is based upon a power of attorney, this must be duly executed and recorded. The examiner must consider whether the date of execution ante-dates the deed executed under it, whether the authority given is broad enough to cover such a deed, whether the wife has joined to authorize the release of dower and homestead, whether the power is signed, sealed and acknowledged so as to be a valid record. If a long time has elapsed between the date of the execution of the power and the date of the deed made under it, inquiry should be made whether the power had been revoked and whether the principal was still living.

Wills.—Almost all titles pass with more or less frequency by will or by descent. In examining transfer by will, the examiner must see that there is a devise covering the property in question. He must further consider many matters such as whether the devisee survived the testator or whether the devise lapsed; whether the will was duly executed and probated, and the nature of the interest or estate given, legal or equitable, present or future. This is often a question of much legal difficulty. Probate proceedings are necessary in most states to the operative effect of a will. An order may be made admitting the will to probate, but such an order may be appealed from or contested within a certain time. The probate of the will does not establish its construction or the nature of the estate taken by the devisee.

Foreign wills, if duly probated in the state of domicile, may usually be recorded if accompanied by a certificate of the judge and clerk of the court where the will was established. Probate proceedings may, however, be necessary in order to determine the claims of creditors in the state. The heir-at-law is presumptive owner, and a purchaser from the heir for value and without notice of the will may in some states get a good title under the recording acts.

Descent.—In case the owner dies without leaving a will, there should be sufficient evidence to establish title by descent. In some states simple proceedings are provided by statute for *prima facie* proof of heirship. To establish satisfactory title of record, however, it is often necessary that there should be complete administration of the intestate's estate. In examining administration proceedings the examiner should consider whether the petition for appointment of administrator was filed by a proper person; whether notice of hearing was given as required; whether notice to creditors of time to file claims against the estate was duly published, and whether the debts and claims presented against the estate have been settled. The proceedings will usually result in a proof or determination of heirship and a decree of distribution to the persons entitled as heirs. It should be considered whether the inheritance tax has been determined and paid.

Liens.—Outstanding encumbrances, such as the lien of mortgages and trust deeds, are common defects, and the lawyer should insist on proper evidence of the extinction of the mortgage. In some cases of old mortgages, where a release or certificate of satisfaction has not been procured, objection may be waived on the ground of the mortgage being barred by the statute of limitations. Among other liens which have to be guarded against are the liens of judgments against the owner of the property, assessments for road and street improvements, legacies charged on the land, mechanics' liens, and tax liens.

It may be well to ascertain whether the vendor owned adjoining houses, and on the sale thereof gave the purchaser implied rights of separate drainage, or rights of way, which would prevent the land retained from being freely built upon.

Execution Sales.—At common law a person relying on a sheriff's deed as a basis of title must produce a valid judgment and a writ of execution authorizing the sale before the sheriff's deed is admissible in evidence to show a transfer of title. Any departure from the statutory requirements as to notice and other steps required in an execution sale may vitiate the sale. The sheriff's deed is merely the last formality in the proceedings and only conveys the interest of the judgment debtor in case the statutory procedure has been fully complied with.

Judicial Sales.—Execution sales are based upon money judgments. Judicial sales, on the other hand, are based upon orders of court directing the sale of designated land. They are usually incidental to some other proceeding, such as administration or the foreclosure of a mortgage. The transfer is complete only when the sale is reported to the court and confirmed or approved by it. Such are sales by executors, administrators and guardians acting under the authority of court. In the examination of a title depending on an execution or judicial sale, every step of the transaction should be carefully scrutinized and the facts of jurisdiction established. The court does not insure the title to real property sold under its decrees.

In examining a transfer by a foreclosure sale, some of the principal questions to be considered as bearing on the validity of the transfer, are as follows: Did the court have jurisdiction of the land? Did it acquire jurisdiction of the parties by service of summons, personally or by publication? Have the statutory requirements for service by publication been followed? Were all parties interested made parties defendant, including the wife of the mortgagor and persons who have acquired any interest subsequent to the mortgage? Does the bill of complaint correctly describe the property? Was a decree properly entered? Was the notice to sell published as required before the time fixed for sale? Were the lands sold as directed, or the sale reported and confirmed? Has the time for redemption expired?

Probate Sales.—While probate sales are frequent links in the chain of title, they are received with extreme suspicion and subject to tests more exacting than other judicial sales. Probate jurisdiction is restricted to particular contingencies, and where there is no power of sale by will, the executor acts simply as officer of the court and must resort to the court for his authority. When an executor is expressly empowered by will to sell the land for any purpose, he may be able to act without order of court.

Tax Deed.—A tax deed is one of the most precarious of all methods of acquiring title. A tax deed has nothing to do with the previous chain of title, but is a grant by the state which extinguishes the old title and all that was dependent upon it. If the land is subject to the taxes and the proceedings are regular, a new and perfect title from the government is established. This title divests all prior liens and encumbrances. A tax title, however, depends upon a strict compliance with the various requirements of the statutes as to time and manner of assessments and sale after notice of delinquency. A certificate of sale is ordinarily issued which vests in the purchaser an equitable interest to get a tax deed and legal title after the period of redemption has expired. The tax deed is merely the last formality in a series of proceedings upon which it depends. It is not in itself evidence of transfer of title, unless by statute its recitals are made *prima facie* evidence that all the proceedings prescribed have been complied with.

It will assist the examiner to prepare a tabulated list of questions, calling attention to the points to be looked out for under the local statutes in examining titles derived through execution sales, foreclosure sales, probate sales, tax sales, and similar proceedings.

SKELETON ABSTRACT OF TITLE
(University of Michigan Law School)
TO

Lots one (1), two (2), nine (9) and ten (10) in block four (4) of Wilson's addition to the city of Blank, in your State.

By direction of James Thompson, Esq., for whom this examination is made, it is assumed that on July 1st, 1881, the title to the fee of the premises described in the above caption was in John Wilson.

John Wilson and Mary, his wife 1. to James Barnes	Mortgage	Dated July 1, 1881. Recorded July 1, 1881, in Book L, p. 280. To secure loan of $30,000, due on or before five years from date. Conveys all of blks. one (1) to ten (10) inclusive, of Wilson's Addition, etc.

Provides for the release of any block upon the payment of $4,000, and of any lot upon the payment of $500.

James Barnes 2. to John Wilson	Release	Dated Dec. 15, 1881. Recorded Dec. 20, 1881, in Book L., p. 850. Releases lots one (1) to five (5) inclusive in block four (4) of Wilson's Addition, etc., from lien of above mortgage.

John Wilson and Mary, his wife 3. to William Adams	Warranty Deed	Dated Dec. 20, 1881. Recorded Dec. 21, 1881, in Book L, p. 900. Consideration $2,000. Conveys lots one (1) and two (2) in block four (4) in Wilson's Addition, etc.

Mary "joins for purpose of releasing her dower in said premises."

William Adams 4. to . Jane Adams, his wife	Quit Claim Deed	Dated Dec. 21, 1881. Recorded Dec. 21, 1881, in Book L, p. 906. Consideration "$1.00 and other considerations."

Conveys an undivided one-half interest in lot two (2) in block (4) in Wilson's Addition, etc.

William Adams and Jane Adams, his wife 5. to James Adams	Warranty Deed	Dated Dec. 21, 1881. Recorded Dec. 21, 1881, in Book L, p. 906. Consideration $1,000. Conveys lot one (1) in block four (4) in Wilson's Addition, etc.

James Barnes 6. to John Wilson	Release	Dated April 10, 1882. Recorded April 10, 1882, in Book N, p. 10. Releases lots six (6) to nine (9) inclusive in block four (4) in Wilson's Addition, etc., from lien of mortgage dated July 1, 1881, and recorded in Book L, at p. 280.

James Adams 7. to Thomas Carter	Mortgage	Dated July 1, 1882. Recorded July 2, 1882, in Book N, p. 250. To secure note of $1,500 due 3 years from date. Conveys lot one (1) in block five (5) of Wilson's Addition, etc.

John Wilson 8. to William Adams	Warranty Deed	Dated April 1, 1881. Recorded August 2, 1882, Book N, p. 511. Consideration $2,000.

Conveys lots nine (9) and ten (10) in block four (4) of Wilson's Addition to the city of Blank.

Thomas Carter 9. to William Adams	Quit Claim Deed	No date. Recorded Sept. 1, 1885, in Book P, p. 255. Conveys lot one (1) in block four (4) in Wilson's Addition, etc.

James Adams and Susan, his wife 10. to Thomas Carter	Warranty Deed	Dated Sept. 2, 1885. Recorded Sept. 2, 1885, in Book P, p. 308. Consideration $500. Conveys lot one (1) in block four (4) of Wilson's Addition, etc., "being the same premises described in a mortgage dated July 1, 1882, and recorded in Book N, at p. 250."

11. [Probate proceedings in the matter of the estate of Jane Adams, deceased, may be assumed to be regular and valid, and to show the following facts: the deceased died April 2d, 1904, leaving surviving her, her husband, William Adams, and three children, Mary Adams Doe, wife of John Doe, Jane Jones, wife of William Jones, and Robert Adams, unmarried; the debts of the estate were all paid from the personal estate, and the balance of such estate was distributed on final order entered July 1st, 1906.]

William Adams 12. to Richard Roe	Quit Claim Deed	Dated Oct. 1, 1910. Recorded same date in Book R, p. 411. Consideration $3,000. Conveys "all my right, title and interest in lots one (1), two (2), nine (9) and ten (10) in block four (4) in Wilson's Addition," etc.

It may be assumed that there is a proper certificate, signed by the abstractors, stating that the foregoing is a complete abstract, and that there are no conveyances, tax sales, or judgments except as therein stated.

DIRECTIONS FOR OPINION

Mr. James Thompson intends to purchase the lands described in the caption above, and retains you to examine the above abstract showing the record title to said lands. Prepare a letter opinion of title, showing in whom the title stands at present, indicating any defects you may find and pointing out the best way of curing them; if you deem any of them unimportant, simply indicate what they are and state that, in your opinion, they may safely be disregarded.

Point out every defect, no matter how slight; any omission in this respect will be counted against you.

Give authority (either statutory or in the cases of your state) for your objections and for your advice to disregard defects.

For the purposes of this paper, you may assume that the present law in your state governs all of the transactions shown in the abstract.

INDEX

—

This l